658.3145   658.31
BAK

Croner's Guide to Handling Sensitive Issues in the Workplace

Nigel L. Baker

Croner Publications Ltd
Croner House
London Road
Kingston upon Thames
Surrey KT2 6SR
Telephone: 0181-547 3333

Copyright © 1997 Croner Publications Ltd

Published by
Croner Publications Ltd
Croner House
London Road
Kingston upon Thames
Surrey KT2 6SR
Tel: 0181-547 3333

All rights reserved.
No part of this publication may be reproduced,
stored in a retrieval system, or transmitted in any form or by
any means, electronic, mechanical, photocopying, recording
or otherwise, without the prior permission of
Croner Publications Ltd.

While every care has been taken
in the writing and editing of this book,
readers should be aware that only Acts of Parliament
and Statutory Instruments have the force of law,
and that only the courts can authoritatively
interpret the law.

British Library Cataloguing-in-Publication Data.
A catalogue record for this book
is available from the British Library.

ISBN 1 85524 452 7

Printed by Clays Ltd, St Ives plc

DE MONTFORT UNIVERSITY
LIBRARY

Date 14/11/97

Loc./Form Riseholme

Class 658.31

Suffix BAK

Contents

Introduction

This reference book is intended for use by managers and supervisory staff who have responsibilities for employees. When dealing with the myriad of sensitive issues which can arise in the workplace, managers need to exercise a variety of key skills, including tact and diplomacy, tolerance, fairness, consistency, good communication and decisiveness.

The success of a business can be affected by the way in which managers handle the difficult and often controversial issues which can frequently arise across a broad front in the workplace. Seemingly everyday matters such as dress and appearance standards can raise passions and preferences in employees, and questions of freedom of the individual are raised by issues such as the regulation of smoking at work.

Protecting staff from harassment can be a difficult job for managers who may need to deal with awkward, embarrassing and often unsubstantiated allegations. Establishing policies on sexual and racial harassment at work is a priority for employers. Discrimination on the grounds of disability is now actionable where the organisation employs 20 or more staff.

Understanding and tolerance are needed in recognising that we live and work in a multi-cultural society where members of different faiths have to interrelate. This can lead to tensions over such things as the timings of holidays and religious observance unless handled sensitively as well as pragmatically by employers.

The use and abuse of drugs and alcohol by job applicants and employees is a challenging but necessary area which management must address because the image, as well as the efficiency of the organisation, can be at stake. Once again, employers should consider introducing policies on such issues.

Ignorance and prejudice surround many attitudes towards individuals who are HIV-positive or who are suffering from AIDS. Employers need to play a part in dispelling some of the myths and fears which abound, in order to ensure that sufferers are not harassed or penalised unfairly in the work context.

Guarding against rising stress levels requires a vigilant approach by managers who need to be able to recognise the warning signs and take swift and decisive action where appropriate.

Dealing with staff who misbehave, either at work or outside it, is an inevitable feature of employing people. Establishing, communicating and enforcing rules of acceptable behaviour for staff is a priority, as is the need to operate a fair disciplinary procedure when dealing with alleged breaches of those rules by employees.

Getting the best out of staff is one of the keys to a successful business. Also vital is dealing with staff who are failing to reach satisfactory standards of work performance. Establishing and communicating what those standards are is an essential task for managers and regular objective monitoring and appraisal of staff is imperative. Where employees are failing to reach standards, help might be required rather than disciplinary measures.

The possibility of deliberate or unconscious ageism being practised by managers against certain individuals is something that requires consideration and action may need to be taken to redress any inequality of opportunity at work.

From the legal standpoint there are many potential pitfalls for the unwary manager. Legal issues can arise when an employer introduces workplace rules for the first time or tries to alter existing rules. Staff who resign because of such changes may claim constructive dismissal or breach of contract, and employees who breach rules might ultimately be dismissed and claim unfair dismissal.

Individuals who feel unable to meet certain pre-employment requirements may present discrimination claims. In discrimination cases, no qualifying service is needed by claimants, the only limit being that a claim must be presented within three months of the act complained of, unless a tribunal considers it is just and equitable to allow an extension or there is an act of continuing discrimination. Tribunals can award successful claimants unlimited compensation in discrimination cases.

Breach of contract claims by employees can also result in compensation being awarded, based on provable loss by the employee. Claims for breach of contract up to £25,000 can be made to industrial tribunals and up to £50,000 to the county court. Employees claiming unfair dismissal generally require two years' continuous service with their employer and claims must also be presented within three months of the effective date of their dismissal. Employees who are dismissed and whose claims succeed can gain re-engagement or reinstatement where suitable. The most common remedy, however, is compensation, which can be up to a maximum of £17,600 for most categories of case.

It should be noted that Legal Aid is not available for industrial tribunal cases. Out-of-court settlements of claims are frequent in sex and race discrimination cases but are also common in unfair dismissal claims through compromise agreements or Advisory, Conciliation and Arbitration Service (ACAS) conciliation.

In adopting effective policies and procedures to deal with sensitive issues in the workplace, the employer not only reduces the likelihood of legal action being brought against it — with the attendant bad publicity — it can also bring about a contented and efficient workforce.

Croner's Guide to Handling Sensitive Issues in the Workplace aims to equip every employer with the necessary information to deal with some of the most challenging problems they will face in the management of people at work.

1. Dress and Appearance

Introduction

The question of codes regulating the dress and appearance of staff is an emotional and controversial one and raises a number of important issues for employers. The employer's right to manage the business in the way it thinks necessary may conflict with individual members of staff's freedom to choose for themselves how to dress and how to judge their own appearance. Employers will need to bear in mind a number of considerations, for example:

- health and safety issues may play a part in what staff wear at work
- an employer may be forced to take a view on the appearance of staff when deciding how to minimise or eliminate the likelihood of workplace harassment
- the imposition of dress codes can have important ramifications in terms of sex and race discrimination claims by staff and in the field of equal opportunities generally.

Once a dress code has been decided upon, there is the question of how to implement it, and to ensure that it has both contractual status and is notified properly to all staff. An employer's disciplinary procedures can be brought into question when dealing with alleged breaches of any dress codes that exist.

Why Have Dress and Appearance Codes?

Rules which try to regulate the dress and appearance of staff are nothing new and are quite widespread throughout industry. According to a survey by Fashionizer, about 50% of employers have some sort of dress code in operation and they are generally supported by staff, with only 17% finding dress codes limiting.

Dress codes can play an important role in projecting a company's image to the general public and hence to its potential customers and clients. This can be achieved by ensuring that staff wear a uniform of some specified description which establishes the corporate identity. In many cases, particularly in the retail and service industries, it is essential that customers can identify an organisation's employees and to distinguish them from members of the public. Similarly, the uniform of the emergency services must be sufficiently distinct for operational reasons and is designed to attract attention. Conveying a professional and business-like impression is a key objective for a variety of organisations, such as banks and building societies, where many, but by no means all, of the staff can have a high public profile.

Staff uniforms can also play an important part in motivating staff by increasing their self-esteem and reinforcing their team spirit. A further benefit is that it can prevent "fashion competitions" at work between staff, which can be both divisive and a considerable distraction to all concerned.

On the other hand, some possible disadvantages of a staff uniform are that it can de-personalise employees and may also make staff feel that they are being forced to wear clothes which are not of their own choice and do not present them at their best.

In some professions, such as nursing, the uniform to be worn by staff is the result of regulations and tradition as well as operational requirements.

There are obvious health and safety reasons why building site workers must wear hard hats while on site and the use of other types of protective equipment, such as goggles, ear protectors and reinforced footwear may all be mandatory in certain working situations.

Where staff are involved in the processing or preparation of food, strict dress codes may dictate that they wear hats, hair nets or snoods from a hygiene point of view.

A 1997 survey by the Aziz Corporation found that 82% of female and 52% of male business people wear a suit to work on most days. Many stated that they took an unfavourable view of staff who dressed casually for business meetings, with 76% of women and 53% of men considering someone wearing casual dress to be "unprofessional and unreliable" or "lacking in respect of business protocol" and only 6% viewed them as modern and uninhibited.

The Scope of Dress Codes

There are a variety of aspects of an employee's overall appearance which an employer might try to regulate. Some rules will relate to particular items of clothing thought to be unacceptable, or compulsory in the case of a uniform, while other rules dictate what is acceptable by way of personal physical appearance. In the latter category, a code could spell out the employer's in-house rules on such aspects as length and colour of hair, make-up, tattoos, jewellery, fingernails and personal hygiene. In relation to clothing, typically there can be rules relating to hem lengths, ties, fashionwear, insignia and badges.

In *Blaik v The Post Office* (COIT 1683/205) it was held to be fair to dismiss an employee who persistently refused to wear a tie during the winter months despite warnings to do so, as part of his employer's "Get Smart" initiative.

In a contrasting decision, in *Greenslade v Hoveringham Gravels* [1975] IRLR 114, it was held to be unfair to dismiss a purchase ledger clerk for not adhering to a requirement to cut his hair and wear a tie. As an employee, he was generally clean and tidy and had almost no contact with the public.

Legal Base

Although employers maintain an inherent right to manage their own businesses, any rules relating to staff conduct must be carefully thought out. It is important to be able to demonstrate a *contractual* right to dictate standards of staff dress and appearance. Terms covering such matters can be either express or implied.

The ideal basis is for the employer to include express written terms relating to dress and appearance in the employee's contract of employment. The detail of the rules can be contained in an employee handbook or code, the contract of employment simply requiring staff to comply with it. Although express terms include oral ones, these are less satisfactory because they can lead to disputes about what was said and when.

When devising express rules governing dress and appearance, the rules should be reasonable, appropriate and clearly understandable by staff. General exhortations that staff should present a "business-like" image are vague and open to interpretation. What constitutes appropriate dress for individual members of staff can vary depending on their role within the organisation and also whether they come into contact with members of the public or customers. In *Eales v Halfords Ltd* (COIT 1179/51), it was held that an employee who worked in a suburban bicycle shop had been unfairly dismissed for contravening a strict dress code when he dyed his hair garishly blond, his working location being contrasted by the tribunal to that of a smart high street jewellers.

Sometimes staff object to a prescribed uniform on the basis that it is inappropriate, as in *Leaper v Delta Hotels Ltd t/a Sheraton Inn* (S/3799/76) in which a female member of staff was held to have been unfairly dismissed for her refusal to wear a cheap, shapeless uniform described as a "peasant girl" outfit. Conversely, a claim by a nurse that the starched cap she had to wear as part of her uniform was demeaning and undignified failed in *Burrett v West Birmingham Health Authority* [1994] IRLR 7.

In *Roberts v Sutcliffe Catering Company (South) Ltd* (COIT 24663/77), it was held that it was fair to dismiss an employee who refused to wear a new set of overalls which were green because she maintained she was superstitious and green was an unlucky colour.

In the absence of any express terms dealing with standards of staff dress and appearance, it might be possible to *imply* terms into the contract. An implied term can arise where it is the subject of a regularly applied practice within an industry or particular trade, or where the individual employer has adopted and maintained a particular practice over a period of time. Equally, an employer might try to argue that it has an implied right to issue lawful and reasonable orders to its staff, who have a corresponding implied duty to follow them.

Communication and Compliance

It is up to the employer to demonstrate that any express contractual rules have been properly communicated to its staff. Simply posting a dress code up on the company noticeboard would not suffice.

Express dress codes need to spell out not only the extent of the rules but also what will happen if staff don't comply with them. Employees should be left in no doubt that a breach of the rules will be treated as a disciplinary matter, with informal and formal procedures to follow. A range of disciplinary sanctions, beginning with warnings, should be highlighted. Time for improvement must be given. An employer must properly investigate complaints and should take into account any explanation or extenuating circumstances put forward by the employee. There may be medical or other personal reasons why the employee came to work as he or she did on the occasion complained of. Counselling or other help may be more appropriate than

9

disciplinary measures; a strict dress code could be relaxed for this employee for a temporary period. However, it is important that dress and appearance codes are normally enforced consistently for all staff otherwise allegations of favouritism, or victimisation, can be levelled against management. If dress and appearance rules are not properly enforced by an employer, they can cease to have binding effect and will fall into disrepute. Where this occurs, it would be necessary to reintroduce the rules and clearly communicate this to all of the staff before acting on them.

A common disciplinary sanction for breach of a dress code is to send the erring employee home to reappear later suitably attired. The employer should expressly reserve the right not to pay the employee for the time spent away, although whether to penalise an employee financially in these circumstances is a matter of discretion for management. Note that an employer's ability to make lawful deductions *from the wages* of staff for acts of misconduct such as these are controlled by **Part II Employment Rights Act 1996**.

Even where there is a comprehensive and detailed code dealing with dress and appearance, it is open to an employer to alter this from time to time in order to reflect changing attitudes and fashions. Variations can easily be implemented where employees' contracts of employment demand compliance with codes contained in their staff handbook, which the employer has a discretion to revise as necessary.

Discrimination Claims

Claims of sex discrimination can arise where different rules regarding dress and appearance are maintained for men and women. This is particularly relevant where there are rules dealing with the length of an employee's hair, what type of clothing is acceptable and the wearing of jewellery, such as earrings. In *Stoke-on-Trent Community Transport v Creswell* (COIT 359/93), the EAT upheld a sex discrimination claim by a woman who was dismissed for wearing trousers to work contrary to an express dress code for female staff. However, it was established in *Smith v Safeway plc* [1996] CA IRLR 456 that an employer *may maintain different dress codes* for men and women at work, providing they enforce a common standard of smartness or conventionality. In *Smith*, this resulted in a male delicatessen employee, who was dismissed when he refused to cut off his pony-tail, losing his claim for sex discrimination even though there were no identical rules for female staff.

Where an employer insists on a particular standard of dress and appearance for staff, this can adversely affect members of certain ethnic groups, whose religious or cultural beliefs may, for instance, stipulate that they don't cut their hair or reveal their head, arms and legs. In these contexts, Sikhs and Muslims could be affected by a uniform or appearance code. In certain working situations special exemptions apply, for example Sikhs with turbans don't have to wear safety helmets on building sites. In jobs where hygiene is critical, an employer may have a "no beards" rule for staff but every effort must be made to accommodate the wishes of individuals from other faiths by seeing whether it is possible to maintain standards of cleanliness by providing them with suitable protective clothing.

Since the introduction of the **Disability Discrimination Act 1995** on 2 December 1996, individuals may complain of discrimination on the grounds of disability against employers with 20 or more staff. Those suffering from a recurring medical condition may not be subjected to a detriment on account of it. For example, an employee who has to wear a uniform made from a particular material which exacerbates a skin complaint that he or she has, will have the right to expect that his or her employer takes reasonable steps to alleviate the difficulty, by either providing a suitable alternative garment or making an exception to the dress code in his or her case.

It should be remembered that, whereas employees require a minimum of two years' continuous service with their employer in order to be eligible to bring a claim for unfair dismissal, no qualifying service is required for discrimination claims and unlimited compensation, which can include an award for injury to feelings, can be awarded by tribunals in successful cases.

Tattoos

Many employers are critical about staff wearing tattoos, whether these be permanent or of a temporary nature, such as transfers. Tattoos are capable of giving a highly visible message or impression and they could affect or influence customers or clients, or the public image of the company. In almost all situations, the impact is perceived by employers as negative and potentially harmful to their business interests.

An employer may dictate in an express and properly communicated dress code, that tattoos are either not to be worn at all or, more likely, are not to be revealed during working hours.

At one stage, it was felt that a ban on tattoos could, in certain circumstances, amount to indirect sex discrimination against men. However, recent research by York University indicates that women are now almost as likely to be tattooed as men — 45% as against 55%. The research also challenges some previous assumptions held about tattoos. In the past, tattoos were apparently linked with aggression and criminal or dysfunctional behaviour. However, in the recent survey, more than 90% of tattoo wearers indicated that they had no criminal record, with only 3.4% of the total having convictions for violent crime. Nearly 87% indicated they had no gang or military membership. In fact, tattoos were just as likely to be sported by doctors, nurses, barristers, middle-aged office workers and civil servants.

Nevertheless, if employers are prejudiced against tattoo wearers, there is nothing to stop them continuing to discriminate against such individuals, either at the point of recruitment or while they are employed by them. But an employer must behave in a consistent manner between the sexes when prohibiting staff wearing tattoos. It would, for instance, be unlawful to take a harsher line with women who have tattoos rather than men, simply because there is a more traditional acceptance of men having them. In *Harris v McDonalds* (COIT 1392/25), it was held to be unlawful sex discrimination to dismiss a female employee who had tattoos on her arms and fingers. Male employees were permitted to have tattoos on their forearms and the tattoos on her fingers were hardly visible to customers, so different standards were being applied.

The introduction of a policy might prove problematic in terms of employees on the staff who already have tattoos. In such cases, insisting on their surgical removal, even while offering to pay the cost, would be viewed as an unreasonable demand and could lead to an unfair dismissal claim, or the employee might resign and claim constructive dismissal. Clearly, such implications need to be thought through by an employer who is considering making a stand on tattoos.

Getting a prominent and highly-visible tattoo could be seen as an act of misconduct where there are existing rules prohibiting it and, in certain situations, it could render an employee incapable of doing the job he or she was employed to do. This could apply, for instance, to a photographic or fashion model whose appearance is of paramount importance to his or her work because a tattoo could limit the variety of work for which he or she was suitable.

Note that although a severe disfigurement is treated as a disability within the **Disability Discrimination Act 1995**, an existing tattoo is not considered to be a condition covered by the Act.

Beards

While not viewed by employers as negatively as tattoos, some employers insist that staff are clean-shaven as part of their dress and appearance codes. Apart from the need to insist on this for hygiene reasons for certain jobs, it would seem to be a difficult rule to justify and may lead to claims of indirect race discrimination from Sikhs, whose religion obliges them to wear beards.

Nevertheless, a recent survey by the Aziz Corporation found that 27% of managers who were surveyed thought that beards looked untidy, 8% said they were "out of place" on businessmen and 7% described them as "unprofessional". A quarter of those with beards thought that they were disadvantageous from a business point of view and none thought it was an advantage.

One problem is what constitutes "a beard", and certain men, with a very rapid growth, might well appear to have "designer stubble" by the middle of the afternoon, even where they have shaved earlier that morning. Special consideration should be given to an employee's personal circumstances, particularly any health factors. In *FME Ltd v Henry* (EAT 874/86), an employee was held to have been unfairly constructively dismissed when, although he had informed his employer that he developed a severe rash if he shaved on a daily basis, he was threatened with being sent home if he arrived at work unshaven.

Jewellery

An employer may stipulate in a dress and appearance code that staff may not wear jewellery to work. Such a rule should be applied equally to men and women and should broadly outline what constitutes "jewellery". In *McConomy v Croft Inns Ltd* [1992] IRLR 561, it was held to be unlawful for the defendants, who were owners of a public house, to exclude a man from admission because he wore earrings, while women were not subject to the same restrictions. Even though this was not an employment law case, this illustrates changing attitudes towards what is acceptable dress for men and women. However, in *Lumber v Hodder* (1991) (unreported), an industrial tribunal held that it was not discriminatory to refuse to allow a man to wear an earring while women were free to do so because female employees were subject to different, but equally restrictive, rules.

Note that there can be health and safety justifications for such rules prohibiting jewellery, for instance the wearing of rings, bracelets, chains or necklaces where machinery is operated. Similarly, in some occupations, hygiene standards can be compromised by the wearing of jewellery. In *Fowler v Fraser t/a Fraser & Williams* (COIT 950/232), an employer failed in his attempt to justify a ban on a male trainee plumber's ear-stud on the grounds of health and safety. Furthermore, it was held that it did not amount to a breach of an implied contractual term on his part.

An employer may insist that jewellery is taken off on arrival but then problems of security can arise if valuable items are left in vehicles or in lockers. Generally speaking, employers tend to discourage employees from bringing valuable personal items to work with them. Furthermore, they can be a distraction to other employees and can start competitions between individuals, each vying to outdo the other.

Again, special care must be taken to avoid potential claims of indirect race discrimination. For instance, orthodox Sikhs wear a Kora, a metal bangle which is a reminder of the unity with God and is a symbol of spiritual allegiance.

Rules about the wearing of jewellery can also cover badges. In some organisations there is a rule that staff must wear identification badges, tags or permits and it can be a disciplinary offence not to do so. Other legitimate rules can prohibit staff from wearing insulting or offensive badges. In *Boychuk v H G Symons Holdings Ltd* [1977] IRLR 395, it was held to be fair to dismiss an employee for wearing a badge stating "Lesbians Ignite" after having been told to remove it. As a ledger clerk, she sometimes came into contact with the public in the course of her work and the EAT held that it was within the employer's discretion to prevent staff wearing a badge or symbol which was likely to cause offence to their colleagues or customers.

In certain occupations, facial body piercing by staff may present an unacceptable image to the public. It is acceptable for an employer to prohibit the wearing of nose studs (and eyebrow, lip and tongue studs or rings) in such occupations. However, even here an employer must act sensitively towards employees of certain cultures such as orthodox married Hindu women who would wish to wear a nose stud to mark their married status.

Decorative and non-medical body piercing is not considered a severe disfigurement within the **Disability Discrimination Act 1995**.

Make-up

An employer may dictate standards of make-up worn by employees. This can include aspects such as lipstick and nail varnish colours. An employer is entitled to consider the image which staff present to customers, clients and the public. However, the situation can be fraught with difficulties. In *Grimston v Initial Health Care* (1994) (unreported), a hospital cleaner at a mental hospital was awarded £1400 by an industrial tribunal for unfair dismissal after she was sacked for wearing too much heavy black eyeliner, which it was alleged could possibly excite patients.

In some occupations there might be a requirement to wear attractive make-up. In *Murphy v Stakis Leisure Ltd* (SCOIT S/0534/89), it was held to be legitimate for the employer to insist that female staff wear make-up and red nail varnish while at work where this helped to create a particular staff image and was balanced by a no-beards rule for male employees.

In some cases, the wearing of perfume could be incompatible with an employee's particular work, for instance in a veterinary surgery where it may cause irritation to the animals.

Safety Equipment

An employer is under a duty to supply appropriate safety equipment for staff and to insist that it is worn at work. Failure to wear protective items, such as: goggles, hard hats, steel toecap shoes, ear defenders, etc, can be expressed in the contract of employment to be an offence of gross misconduct leading to summary dismissal.

However, an employer should always investigate the reasons put forward by an employee who is refusing to wear safety equipment. In *BAC Ltd v Austin* [1978] IRLR 332, an employee was held to have been unfairly constructively dismissed for not wearing the issued safety goggles because she couldn't wear them over her glasses. The employers had failed to investigate what was a reasonable complaint and to consider how they could surmount her difficulties.

Similarly, an employee cannot be penalised for not working where the employer fails to provide appropriate protective equipment. In *Kirkcaldy District Council v Baxter* (EAT 540/78), it was held that it was unreasonable for the council to insist that a refuse collector continued to do his rounds in driving rain without adequate waterproof protective clothing.

Personal Hygiene

An employer may have express rules covering the personal hygiene of staff. The problem caused by unpleasant body odours can be a serious one where employees work in close proximity, in confined spaces, or need to work in close consultation while in teams. If colleagues find it too unpleasant to work closely with someone because the individual smells or has bad breath, this can seriously disrupt workplace efficiency.

An employer needs to carefully investigate such complaints and needs to do so in a delicate and sensitive manner. The employee in question may be unaware that he or she is causing a problem and could be embarrassed or feel inadequate. There may be several easily correctable explanations for the problem, such as the lack of a deodorant or a failure to wash or to change clothes regularly enough. Failure by the employee to respond to these remedial measures may lead to disciplinary action being taken against him or her.

If the cause relates to a medical problem, such as profuse sweating, then an employer should not only act in a sympathetic way, but treat the matter as a capability issue and provide help and assistance, including counselling and medical help.

Under the guidance notes issued by the Secretary of State under s.3 of the **Disability Discrimination Act 1995**, an industrial tribunal should take into account, in determining the question of "disability", the fact that an employee is inclined to neglect basic functions, which includes his or her personal hygiene.

Summary

- Approximately half of all employers apply some form of dress code to their employees.

- The imposition of dress codes can have ramifications on personal freedom, sex and race discrimination and equal opportunities.

- The provision of a uniform projects a corporate image, helps customers distinguish employees from members of the public and reduces competition between staff.

- Staff dress may be influenced by tradition, hygiene and health and safety considerations.

- Rules on dress and appearance should be reasonable, appropriate and clearly understandable by staff.

- It is the employer's responsibility to ensure that rules are properly communicated to staff.

- When dealing with alleged breaches of their dress and appearance code, employers must follow a fair disciplinary process.

2 Harassment and Bullying at Work

Nature and Scope of Harassment

Harassment can be defined as inappropriate behaviour, actions, comments or physical contact that is objectionable or causes offence. It is any unwanted conduct which is offensive to the recipient. While the most common forms of workplace harassment involve sexual and racial harassment, there may be a range of different types of unacceptable conduct. These can relate to sex, race, age, disability, religion, and sexual orientation. In all these situations, harassment can arise where the conduct towards another is intimidating, annoying, hurtful, or malicious and is unwelcome and unreciprocated. Harassment of any kind is essentially an attack on someone's dignity as an individual.

Harassment may take any of the following forms of behaviour:
- verbal
- non-verbal
- physical
- other.

Verbal harassment would include offensive remarks, personal comments and innuendos. Non-verbal harassment would encompass exposure to literature, photographs, graffiti and pin-ups. Physical harassment typically involves some element of bodily contact or touching. Other forms of harassment can include unwelcome gifts and practical jokes at another's expense.

The Royal Mail defines harassment in its company statement as:

any conduct related to age, creed, disability, nationality, race, religion, sex, sexual orientation or any other personal

> *characteristic which is unwanted by the recipient, or any
> such conduct based on the above characteristics which
> affects the dignity of any individual or group of individuals
> at work. Harassment may be persistent or an isolated
> incident, and may be directed towards one or more
> individuals.*

Harassment is not only unwelcome physical contact, assault or propositions. It includes suggestive remarks or gestures, pin-ups, graffiti, offensive comments, jokes and banter on race, religion, sex or other personal characteristics. None of these is part of a culture in which all employees and groups of employees are treated with dignity and respect.

Why Should an Employer be Concerned About Workplace Harassment?

1. It is a form of misconduct by an employee.
2. It is frequently an abuse of delegated power.
3. It is behaviour which pollutes the workplace and is therefore a health and safety issue.
4. It is bad for business in terms of recruitment and retention of staff.
5. It opens the employer up to legal claims by staff who suffer harassment.
6. It is evidence of a lack of equal opportunities at the workplace and a failure to follow good business practice.

Criminal Responsibility

Under s.154 of the **Criminal Justice and Public Order Act 1994**, a new criminal offence of "intentional harassment" was created. The police have an immediate power of arrest under this Act. An individual will be convicted if the prosecution are able to prove beyond reasonable doubt that the defendant was guilty of intentionally harassing, and that the victim was actually harassed, alarmed or distressed.

The Act defines harassment as "the use of threatening, abusive or insulting words or behaviour, or disorderly behaviour". This could also arise through the display of writing, signs or other visible representations which are threatening, abusive or insulting. The maximum penalty under the Act is six months' imprisonment or a £5000 fine.

It would be easy for the prosecution to prove intention where the defendant is shown to have been previously warned about the behaviour which was causing distress. As with any potentially criminal behaviour engaged in by staff at work, employers have an important role to play in preventing it, together with a direct interest in doing so.

An IRS survey in 1996 investigated the reasons why employers tackled harassment in the workplace with the following findings:

- the need to ensure equal opportunities at work — 95% of employers
- in order to avoid legal action and potential costs, such as increased absenteeism, higher sickness levels and lower productivity — 66% of employers
- as a response to European Union developments — 18% of employers
- as an aid to recruitment and selection —14% of employers.

What Effect Can Harassment Have on the Recipient?

The victims of harassment may suffer a range of adverse consequences.

1. It can cause symptoms of anxiety, tension, irritability, depression and stress.
2. It can demotivate, humiliate and demean them.
3. It can result in increased absence rates.
4. It can affect their promotion prospects and/or their job security.
5. It can cause staff to resign from their jobs.

Sexual Harassment

What is Sexual Harassment?

Sexual harassment is when a person experiences hurtful and belittling behaviour because of his or her sex. It can be described as any unwanted and unwelcome sexual comments, looks, actions, suggestions or physical contact which are found objectionable and as a result of which an employee's job security, job performance or job prospects are threatened or an unpleasant or intimidating working environment is created.

According to a 1996 IRS survey, 65% of organisations in the private sector operate a sexual harassment policy, as compared with only 20% in 1992.

Sexual harassment at work is widespread and is damaging people and organisations on a huge scale, according to The Industrial Society's Survey *No Offence* (1993). The survey of almost 2000 people suggested that more than half of working women and 7% of men have been the victim of sexual harassment at work.

The effects on the victims included reduced productivity, interference with thinking and judgment, an inability to concentrate, depression and mood swings, absenteeism and lateness. It therefore affects both performance and job satisfaction. As a result 10% of the victims left, transferred or said they were denied career moves.

Only 5% complained through their employer's grievance procedure but more than 75% of those who did, reported an improvement.

In 1991, the European Union published a Code of Practice on measures to combat sexual harassment as part of its Recommendations on *Dignity at Work*. Although the code is not legally binding, it was stated in *Wadman v Carpenter Farrer Partnership* [1993] IRLR 374 that it provided useful guidance for industrial tribunals when considering allegations of sexual harassment.

In July 1996, the EU Commission stated that it was its future intention to legislate to provide a framework of minimum standards for employers to follow in order to eliminate sexual harassment at work. This is because the EU considers that existing legislation in the Member States is generally inadequate to ensure a working environment free from sexual harassment.

Under the code, "sexual harassment" is defined as:

unwanted conduct of a sexual nature, or other conduct based on sex affecting the dignity of women and men at work.

Conduct is unacceptable if it is:

unwanted, unreasonable and offensive to the recipient

and/or the conduct creates

an intimidating, hostile or humiliating working environment for the recipient.

"Unwanted" means uninvited, unwelcome and unreciprocated.

A key feature of the definition is that the behaviour is *unreciprocated*. A flirtation based on mutual consent and attraction is not sexual harassment. Normal social interaction at work can be conducive to a positive working environment and it is only when there is the imposition of unwelcome attention by one person on another that harassment arises.

Note that in *Wileman v Minilec Engineering Ltd* [1988] IRLR 144, it was held that it doesn't matter whether remarks or actions were not meant to be offensive. If the complainant found them offensive, that constitutes harassment.

UNISON states that sexual harassment is:

any unwanted conduct of a sexual nature which is offensive to the recipient and includes leering or gesturing; the display of offensive materials; suggestive remarks; "jokes" or personal comments; sexual propositions, threats or personal comments; and physical contact, from touching to rape.

In 1994, British Rail issued guidelines to its staff on sexual harassment. Employees can be disciplined for unwanted physical conduct, which includes insulting and abusive behaviour. Under its policy, sexual misconduct includes:

> *unwelcome advances, patronising nicknames or titles, propositions or remarks, innuendo, lewd comments and repeated suggestions for unwanted social activities both in and out of the workplace.*

A litmus test for sexual harassment based on the following questions has been drawn up in the US.

1. Would you say or do this in front of your spouse/parents?
2. Would you say or do this in front of a colleague of the same sex?
3. Would you like your behaviour reported in the local paper?
4. Does the behaviour in question need to be said or done at all?

Sex Discrimination Act 1975

"Sexual harassment" is not specifically mentioned in the **Sex Discrimination Act 1975**. However, it was established in *Strathclyde Regional Council v Porcelli* [1986] IRLR 134 that it is a form of sex discrimination. It constitutes "less favourable treatment" on the grounds of sex and causes the complainant a "detriment". In *Porcelli*, Mrs Porcelli was sexually harassed by two male colleagues who wanted her to leave her job. They brushed up against her and made suggestive remarks. This was viewed as unfavourable treatment *based on her sex* and was more than simply unpleasant behaviour to which a man could have objected.

Note that it is possible to claim sexual harassment against someone of the same sex. In *Gates v Security Express Guards* (COIT 45142/92), an industrial tribunal awarded a male employee £4500 compensation because of sexual harassment by his male boss and in *Tuohy v Stoneham, Langham &*

Passmore (1995) (unreported), a legal secretary who was sacked after complaining she was being sexually harassed by her lesbian boss was awarded £7527 compensation by a tribunal.

Apart from internal sanctions applied by an employer against the perpetrator for proven harassment, the victim may sue for compensation. Note that action may also be taken vicariously against the employer as well as the culprit. Under s.41(3) of the **Sex Discrimination Act 1975**, employers have a defence against claims of sexual harassment where they can show that they have taken "such steps as were reasonably practicable" to prevent their employee from committing a discriminatory act of sexual harassment. Note however that employers are finding it difficult to succeed with this defence — see cases later.

In *Waters v Commissioner of Police of the Metropolis* [1995] ICR 510, it was held that an employee had no protection against victimisation by the employer in respect of an act of sexual harassment by a work colleague while they were both off duty at a police section house. This was because the act was not done in the course of employment. However, the decision in *Jones v Tower Boot Co. Ltd* [1996] IRLR 727 now casts doubt on this decision.

An Employer's Responsibilities

Employers are under a duty to safeguard the welfare of their employees. Sexual harassment should be seen as a form of misconduct to which the employer's disciplinary procedures are applicable.

Employers should implement policies designed to demonstrate their concern and commitment over the issue. Positive duties should be placed on managers and supervisors to implement the policy and enforce it.

Policy statements must clearly indicate the procedures which should be followed in the event of a complaint of sexual harassment being made. Employers must be ready to act regardless of any formal complaint being made if the circumstances permit.

In *Mullan v Department of Employment* (COIT 20113/90), it was held that the employer was liable because the nine month delay in dealing with the complaint in question was too long a period.

Having devised a policy, it is essential that it is properly and effectively communicated to all staff, eg by circulars, notices, team briefings and in contracts of employment.

There should be specially trained staff designated to receive complaints. Training should also be given to all managers and supervisors. There should be an informal resolution procedure, separate from the grievance procedure, and it is important that there is a proper system of investigation, which must be followed once a complaint is lodged. Counsellors should be available to talk with harassed staff.

The normal features of a disciplinary system must be adhered to, namely:

- notice of allegation
- right to be accompanied
- right to be heard and respond, etc.

Records must be kept of meetings and investigations. Where allegations are proven disciplinary sanctions should be applied, eg disciplinary transfer. Note that sexual harassment can constitute gross misconduct. The sexual harassment policy should outline the possible disciplinary penalties.

Employers must monitor and review their sexual harassment policies to ensure they are operating effectively, and trade unions also have an important part to play in preventing harassment at work.

In *Goold (Pearmak) Ltd v McConnell* [1995] IRLR 516, it was held that an employer's failure to provide employees with a proper method of dealing with work-related grievances was a breach of an implied term of their contracts of employment. The employees were therefore entitled to resign and claim constructive dismissal. In the context of sexual harassment, this case reinforces the duty on employers to take employees' complaints seriously and to provide a mechanism for dealing with them.

In *Dillon v Outline Engraving Co. Ltd* (COIT 18526/93), it was held that an employer has an obligation to provide an environment free of sexual harassment and a system whereby an employee can complain of behaviour which is unwanted, offensive and humiliating.

Good practice in dealing with sexual harassment means employees should:
- have a policy and a procedure
- communicate the policy to all staff
- have specifically trained staff to deal with complaints
- train all managers and supervisors in dealing with harassment
- have an informal resolution procedure
- have counsellors available for harassed staff.

Recent Cases on Sexual Harassment

Rosse v Paramount House Group Ltd (1994) (unreported)
An instruction by her employer for a woman to attend meetings at which women were sexually harassed was potentially sex discrimination and her dismissal for refusing to attend was potentially unfair because of this.

Insitu Cleaning Ltd v Heads [1994] IRLR 4
An employee was held to have been unlawfully discriminated against when her manager said, "hiya big tits" to her when he entered a meeting. A single act such as this can be "unwanted behaviour".

The EAT issued the following guidance to employers.
1. Companies should adopt a separate procedure dealing exclusively with complaints of sexual harassment.

2. The procedure should contain an informal first step enabling complaints to be dealt with sympathetically before matters get out of hand.
3. Any complaint should be dealt with from the perception of the person aggrieved.

Wildman v Clyde & Co. (1994) (unreported)

A £20,000 out-of-court settlement was made to their former marketing manager by a London law firm. She resigned after her complaints about an intense campaign of sexual harassment by a colleague were ignored.

Hillen v Tuke (1995) (unreported)

An 18 year old trainee pilot who was forced to leave her job after she spurned the sexual advances of her 63 year old flying instructor was awarded £21,500 in damages. The award included £15,000 for injury to feelings, £1000 aggravated damages and £1500 for financial loss.

Hoyle v Gill (1996) (unreported)

A 32 year old part-time barmaid who resigned after being repeatedly taunted about the size of her breasts by her employer was awarded £2400 compensation. He had suggested that she should have breast implants or put socks into her bra to improve her figure. This verbal abuse lasted for two years.

White v Metropolitan Police (1996) (unreported)

A police sergeant was found to have been sexually discriminated against by the Metropolitan Police after a female officer made "wholly unjustified" claims of sexual harassment against him. He was awarded £16,200 compensation, plus £28,200 costs. Following the allegation against him, he was transferred, giving the clear impression that he was in the wrong. The industrial tribunal held that a woman would not have been so treated.

Scanlon v Liverpool City Council (1996) (unreported)

A female council worker who was subjected to a campaign of sexual harassment by her clerk of works was awarded £3300 for injury to feelings and £1915 for her unfair constructive dismissal. She had been addressed as "babe", touched and been made to work in an intimidating environment.

McIntyre v Thomas Jones Associates (1996) (unreported)

A young woman office worker who suffered daily sexual harassment involving photographs, sex jibes and abuse was awarded £3664 compensation by a tribunal.

Poole v BUPA (1996) (unreported)

A £10,000 out-of-court settlement was given to a 22 year old former saleswoman who claimed that she had been sexually harassed and humiliated by her female boss and then dismissed because she complained.

Lawton v Greene (1996) (unreported)

An £8350 award was made to a hotel assistant who was sexually harassed by her boss over a six-year period. This had consisted of remarks, propositions, innuendos and touching.

Go Kidz Go Ltd v Bourdouane [1996] IDS Brief, 578

A company which provided children's parties on a commercial basis was held to have discriminated against a female employee on the grounds of sex when, following a complaint by her that she was sexually harassed by a parent at a children's birthday party she was hosting, the employer failed to take all reasonable steps to protect her from further harassment. Note that the case did not say that the employer was vicariously liable for the acts of a third party. The employers were personally liable because of the way they handled her complaints about being harassed by someone who was not an employee. Once they had learned of her complaint, her employers were in a position to prevent it happening or continuing.

Morris v MOD (1997) (unreported)

A wren who suffered years of sexual bullying and taunts from her colleagues and which resulted in her depression and discharge from the Navy was awarded £65,000 by a tribunal.

Ashurst and Rose v North Yorkshire Police (1996) (unreported)

In September 1996, North Yorkshire Police disclosed that they had paid an out-of-court settlement of more than £110,000 to two female officers to settle their sexual harassment claims.

Clayton v Hereford & Worcester Fire Station (1997) (unreported)

In March 1997, an out-of-court settlement of £200,000 was paid to a former fire officer who had suffered years of harassment at the hands of her male colleagues at the fire station, and which ultimately led to her resignation.

Harassment Checklist

The following is a summary of steps for employers to take in dealing with sexual harassment.

1. Develop a policy statement which prohibits sexual harassment.
2. Develop clear and fair procedures to deal with any complaints or allegations of sexual harassment.
3. Publicise the policy and procedures to all employees and monitor the effectiveness of these.
4. Provide training for all supervisors, managers and employees on the issues surrounding sexual harassment and how to recognise it as unacceptable behaviour.
5. Ensure that adequate internal communication exists together with proper support systems.

Employers would also be well advised to include special e-mail clauses in their sexual harassment policies. E-mail harassment can arise through repeated or unwanted requests or messages containing sexual innuendos or pictures. If this is done at work, or on office equipment, the employer could be jointly responsible unless it has taken all reasonable steps to prevent such harassment. This applies whether or not the e-mail is sent with the employer's knowledge or approval.

In *Morse v Future Reality* (1996) (unreported), a tribunal made a £22,000 award to a computer executive who resigned from her £60,000 job as a result of a stream of pornographic images with which she was bombarded from the internet by her male colleagues.

In 1997, NatWest Markets dismissed 3 employees and disciplined 12 others for distributing pornography on the company's e-mail system.

Racial Harassment

Race Relations Act 1976

Racial harassment and abuse at work constitute "less favourable treatment" in which the individual suffers "a detriment", within the Act. A "detriment" includes an insult but can also include blocked promotion, unfavourable transfers, unfair selection for redundancy and dismissal.

In *Ratanshi v British Rail Engineering* (unreported), Mr R was called a "black bastard" to his face by his supervisor. This was held to be an unlawful discriminatory detriment.

In *Deson v BL Cars Ltd* (EAT 173/80), Mr Deson was held to have been discriminated against when he was moved to a different machine in order to preserve the industrial peace by separating him from a racist worker. Although there was no loss of pay or status, there was a "detriment" because the work to which he was transferred was considered less interesting and attractive.

In *De Souza v Automobile Association* [1986] IRLR 103, it was held that a racist insult could constitute a "detriment", as could stressful working conditions generally if caused by racial harassment.

Under the Act, complainants may argue either direct or indirect discrimination. Additionally, claimants have the right not to be victimised at work for pursuing their rights under the **Race Relations Act 1976** (RRA).

Although legal aid is not available for industrial tribunal claims, the Commission for Racial Equality (CRE) or any relevant trade union may provide financial assistance or representation to pursue a claim.

What is Harassment?

There is no hard and fast definition of racial harassment. It is a general term covering a wide range of unacceptable, and often unlawful, behaviour.

Racial harassment can be defined as any unwanted and unwelcome terms, comments, actions or behaviour relating to race, which members of a racial, cultural or religious group find abusive, offensive or insulting, and as a result of which an employee's job security is threatened or an intimidating working environment is created.

The Chair of the CRE stated:

For anyone who is a target of harassment, being at work means being in a permanent state of dread, being unable to concentrate, and failing to realise one's full potential. Worse, tension is contagious and invariably affects others, with ultimately damaging consequences for the organisation as a whole.

Employers are under a legal and moral duty to ensure that their employees do not have to suffer the indignity and humiliation of racial harassment.

The TUC defines racial harassment as:

– abusive language and racist "jokes"

- racial name-calling
- display of racially-offensive written or visual material including graffiti
- physical threats, assault and insulting or abusive behaviour or gestures
- open hostility to black workers including organised hostility in the workplace
- unfair allocation of work and responsibilities
- exclusion from normal workplace conversation or social events, ie being "frozen out".

The CRE describes the following as examples of the subtler forms of harassment:

- racist jokes
- banter
- insults
- taunts
- jibes
- literature
- graffiti
- shunning people because of their race, colour, nationality or ethnic background
- excluding them from conversations
- making racist insinuations
- being condescending or deprecating about the way they dress or speak
- picking on them unnecessarily.

Racial harassment reinforces segregation and isolation in the workplace.

Racial harassment need not be deliberate or conscious and it is no defence to say "I meant no offence" or "it was only a joke".

When employers get complaints of racial harassment they need to view them from the perception of the complainant, and the test is not what a bystander might think.

There is a business case for eliminating racial harassment in the workplace. Racial harassment can cause damage, tension and conflict in the workplace. It can lead to:

- poor morale
- increased staff turnover
- decreased productivity
- decreased efficiency
- divided teams.

Liability for Racial Harassment

Under s.32(1) of the **Race Relations Act 1976** (RRA) an employer can be vicariously liable for harassment occurring in the workplace, as well as the culprit being personally liable for their actions. However, the fact that an employee commits an act of discrimination at work does not *automatically* make the employer vicariously liable: the employee must have been *acting in the course of his or her employment* when the discrimination occurred.

Jones v Tower Boot Co. Ltd [1996] IRLR 727
The employee was subjected to dreadful racial harassment including being branded with a screwdriver and whipped. The Court of Appeal held that an employer could be vicariously liable for the racially abusive acts of one of their employees even though the acts in question were not connected with acts authorised to be done as part of his work. The words "in the course of his employment" in the RRA were not to be construed restrictively in this context.

Bee v White and Dodd t/a Five Minute Car Wash (1994) (unreported)
The company was ordered to pay Mr Bee £2766 compensation because he was subjected to a battery of increasingly provocative racial insults by other employees during the two months he worked at the defendants and his supervisor viewed the racial insults as nothing more than

banter, even though they eventually made the complainant ill.

Bryans v Northumberland College (1995) (unreported)
Mr Bryans was awarded £30,000 compensation because he was the victim of a continuing stream of racial abuse from some of his colleagues because he was Irish.

Defences

It is no defence for an employer to say it didn't know about the harassment or wouldn't have approved of the harassment if it had known about the harassment.

Under s.32(3) of the RRA an employer's only defence is to show that it has taken reasonably practicable steps to prevent racial harassment. The cases of *Dias* and *Wilson* illustrate the difficulty with which employers are finding it to succeed with the defence.

Graham v Royal Mail and Nicolson (1993) (unreported)
The company had fully investigated an incident of racial abuse and had transferred the culprit to another department and given him a warning in accordance with its procedures on harassment. The tribunal was of the view that there was nothing else that the employer could have done.

Wilson v J Sainsbury plc (COIT 7957/94)
The employer was found liable for racial harassment because there was "no evidence of formal training in equal opportunities…and the management were just not trained to deal with the situation that arose, either speedily or effectively".

Dias v Avon County Council (COIT 9660/94)
Although the employer had an equal opportunities policy and had carried out training for the managers, the industrial tribunal decided that it had not taken such steps as were reasonably practicable, which means doing more than the minimum that a reasonable employer would do. On balance,

it was held that the employer had not met the strict requirements of s.32(3).

Recent Cases on Racial Harassment

Following a successful claim, an industrial tribunal can make recommendations as to what steps an employer must take to deal with harassment, and within what timescale. If an employer has a policy, it must be effective.

Cooley v British Road Services Ltd (COIT 2880/94)
Mr Cooley was subjected to racial jibes while he was working as a traffic controller in the BRS Oxford depot. The BRS disciplinary guidance book itself stated that, "harassment may take the form of ridicule, comments about appearance, patronising remarks or embarrassing jokes." At first when he complained he was told to "forget it" and following a subsequent complaint he was told that no action would be taken because the jokes were not malicious. The industrial tribunal awarded him £2240 compensation, which included £1000 for injury to feelings.

Johnson v Armitage, Marsden & HM Prison Service [1996] TLR 31
A black prison officer who was subjected to a campaign of appalling treatment over a two year period was awarded a total compensation of £28,500. He had been manhandled and ostracised by his colleagues. The award was made up of £20,000 for injury to his feelings as against the Prison Service, £500 against each of two prison officers personally, plus an award of £7500 aggravated damages.

Francique v Colne Valley Spinning Co. Ltd (1996) (unreported)
A 60 year old black employee with 28 years' service with the company was held to have been unlawfully dismissed for a false reason having complained that he was the victim of repeated racial abuse from his workmates, which his employers had ignored. He was awarded £32,000 compensation by a tribunal.

Burton & Rhule v De Vere Hotels [1996] IRLR 596

Two black waitresses succeeded in their claim that their employer had failed to protect them from racist jokes told by Bernard Manning at a dinner at which they were serving. The tribunal held that an employer subjects an employee to the detriment of racial harassment if it causes or permits the racial harassment to occur in circumstances in which it can control whether it happens or not.

Baptiste v Bradford Telegraph & Argus (1996) (unreported)

A job applicant who was told in an interview that being called a "black bastard" was typical office banter, was awarded £13,000 in compensation.

Firdous v Bethlem & Maudsley NHS Trust (1996) (unreported)

A record settlement of £50,000 was reached in the case of a Pakistani-born nurse who was hounded by her white boss for 12 months, during which time it was alleged that her complaints were not taken seriously by management.

How to Prevent Racial Harassment at Work

It is dangerous for employers to assume that there is no problem in the workplace simply because there have been no complaints about harassment from employees. There could be many reasons for this, for instance:

- individuals may be afraid of retaliation or reprisals
- individuals may feel too intimidated to act
- individuals may not want to make a fuss, especially if they think they won't be believed or understood
- individuals may feel that no action will be taken about their complaints
- individuals may not know how to go about making a complaint. This is particularly important where the allegation of harassment is being levelled against their own line manager or supervisor.

Employers should adopt a harassment policy together with procedures for dealing with alleged breaches of the policy. It is important that such policies are effectively communicated to all staff, ideally on induction. Trade union involvement here can be beneficial. The message needs to be reinforced as frequently as possible, eg in company annual reports, staff newsletters and training. Staff should be fully aware that racial harassment is a disciplinary issue and constitutes gross misconduct for which the likely penalty is dismissal without notice.

Eradication of harassment in the workplace is the responsibility of all staff, so those who witness the harassment of others should be prepared to take the necessary action to report it.

Small firms also require harassment policies and are in a better position to monitor precisely what is going on in their workplaces.

All staff should receive training to ensure that the organisation's racial harassment policy is effective. They should be fully aware of what constitutes harassment and how to spot it. Line managers and supervisors have a particular responsibility in this regard and should receive further training, dealing with such matters as racial awareness, the law on harassment and discrimination and how to investigate and deal with complaints.

Bowen v Bradmeres Engineering Ltd (1993) (unreported)

Mr Bowen, who was of mixed race, was a fitter and supervisor at Bradmeres Ltd. His managing director made racially offensive remarks in his presence and refused to apologise for them. A fellow director told Mr Bowen that racially offensive behaviour was acceptable within the engineering industry and that he would have to "grin and bear it". When Mr Bowen refused to work with his manager, he was demoted and later sacked. The industrial tribunal awarded Mr Bowen £2500 damages for injury to his feelings, partly because of the inept and offensive way in which Mr

Bowen's disciplinary hearing was conducted, together with £9009 damages for unfair dismissal.

How to Deal With Complaints of Racial Harassment at Work

Employers should treat all complaints of harassment seriously and sympathetically and take prompt action.

A racial harassment policy should spell out how complaints will be dealt with. The following points should be considered.

1. Procedures should be sufficiently clear to ensure that those wishing to complain know what to do and whom to approach.

2. Individuals should be given contact points or designated officers to whom they can turn for informal resolution of a problem. Such discussions must be confidential.

3. The policy should set time limits for each stage of investigation which can be either formal or informal, dependent on how the complainant wants to proceed. If informal action is sought, trained counsellors can be useful in pinpointing and solving the problem at this stage.

4. Where formal action is unavoidable:
   - individuals should know how to make a formal complaint in writing, identifying the harasser
   - time limits should be set for settling complaints swiftly and decisively (in *Clarke v BTR Fatati Ltd* (1992) (unreported), it was held that one month was too long)
   - complaints should be formally acknowledged in writing and full written details and notification should also be given to the alleged harasser
   - confidentiality must be maintained
   - complainants must not be victimised in any way while the matter is being investigated and should

receive full support from the employer while properly using the harassment procedure

- ideally, complaints of harassment should have their own procedure separate to the normal grievance procedure
- complaint hearings should be convened as quickly as possible by an independent person or panel of unconnected employees:
  - such individuals should be fully trained in handling complaints of racial discrimination or harassment
  - the normal rules of natural justice apply to such hearings since they are in the disciplinary field
  - complaints must be proven on the balance of probabilities
- both complainant and alleged harasser should be allowed representation and/or interpreters
- both the complainant and defendant should receive a decision in writing following the hearing and any disciplinary penalties should follow as quickly as possible — if the parties are to be separated, it is the *harasser* who should be moved, transferred or suspended, not the complainant
- in order to prevent further harassment, the complainant should receive a written undertaking that he or she will not suffer further detriment and will not be victimised.

It is important that employers monitor and review the effectiveness of their own harassment policies. This is an ongoing process. It is also useful evidence to prove that an employer has been effective in detecting and dealing with harassment in the workplace.

Employers' harassment policies should also cover the possibility that their contractors, customers or clients might racially harass employees and that this will not be tolerated.

Bullying at Work

Over the last decade, bullying at work has become an issue for employers which has resulted in many firms devising policies for staff both as potential victims and culprits.

Bullying can take many forms but is a type of misconduct and should ultimately be dealt with as a disciplinary matter. Bullying involves intentional intimidation or belittling of an individual and may arise from the misuse of managerial status or simply as a result of certain physical and mental characteristics.

In *Brearley v William Morrisons plc* (COIT 3073/168B) the employee was subjected to a campaign of bullying by his manager who referred to him sarcastically as "brain dead" and "illiterate". He also suffered various physical assaults, including having cleaning agent put into his tea. These antics were described as "an extremely bad case of bullying, harassment and humiliation".

In *Hatrick v City Fax* (COIT 3041/138H) an employee was held to have been unfairly dismissed when she left after having had her hair forcibly cut by her colleagues. This was described as a "blatant case of horseplay or bullying".

In *Evans v Sawley Packaging Co. Ltd* (COIT 2916/185E) it was held that the employer was vicariously liable for the behaviour of the staff in carrying out a series of violent actions against the employee because the employer had taken no steps to prevent the bullying and was therefore in breach of his duty to provide a safe working environment.

The effects of such behaviour can be quite serious and apart from reducing efficiency levels at work, it can ultimately cause a resignation if not handled properly by management. In *Robinson v Hallowes Golf Club* (1996) (unreported), an industrial tribunal awarded a dyslexic golf club greenkeeper £8819 compensation for being bullied by his manager for four years because of his condition.

In 1994, the BBC commissioned two surveys into bullying at work. Of the personnel heads questioned, 75% reported recognising bullying at work to be a potential problem.

Of the employees questioned, 78% said that they had witnessed bullying at work and 50% said that they themselves had been bullied at some time.

Bullying is a significant cause of stress in an organisation and is often confused with a way of motivating staff, especially in highly competitive commercial markets. Much of this is counter-productive if the employees in question have increased absenteeism rates, loss of morale and lack of ambition as a result.

The white-collar union MSF has urged employers to act against workplace bullies, and trade unions generally are keen to co-operate with management to devise and implement workplace policies. The MSF survey found that 22% of organisations had a policy for dealing with bullying.

The MSF union has adopted the following definition of bullying:

Persistent, offensive, abusive, intimidating, malicious or offensive behaviour, abuse of power or penal sanctions, which make the recipient feel upset, threatened, humiliated or vulnerable, which undermines their self-confidence and which may cause them to suffer stress.

MSF are sponsoring a private member's bill to outlaw bullying at work and the existence of an anti-bullying policy would be a defence against legal action. Such a policy should provide:

- a formal and informal means of complaint
- a requirement for confidentiality
- a procedure for investigating the incident
- a series of disciplinary sanctions to be used against perpetrators.

At a conference in September 1995, it was stated that a third to a half of work-related stress is caused by bullying. For an individual business, stress-related problems could absorb the equivalent of 5%–10% of profits. MSF has also begun proceedings against the insurance firm CIS for the alleged psychological and physical damage caused to one employee by a manager claimed to have a long track record of bullying. Twenty three staff have complained that the manager in question had verbally abused and mistreated them for more than two years and five of the staff had taken stress-related sick leave as a result.

An NAS/UWT survey in 1995 found that bullying amongst teachers was an "epidemic", with 100,000 victims of colleagues' sarcasm, intimidation and occasional assaults.

A study in 1996 by Charlotte Rayner estimated the cost of bullying bosses to be £4 billion a year in lost labour, based on the number of employees forced to go home or to seek legal redress. More than half of respondents had been bullied; male managers were twice as likely as female managers to bully, but female managers were three times as likely to bully other women staff than men were.

How to Deal With Complaints of Racial Harassment at Work

As with any workplace issue, a proper investigation must be made into any complaint of bullying. Complaints will only surface if employees have confidence in the system and know that allegations will not be ridiculed or held against the complainant.

Complaints should first be dealt with informally and may involve a line manager as an intermediary. Where this proves impractical or unsuccessful, the employee may utilise the grievance procedure or specific procedure established for complaints of bullying.

Investigations into bullying often bring to light underlying problems such as clash of personalities, incompetence, power struggles and job insecurity.

As independent corroboration will be rare and witnesses usually thin on the ground, it is important for victims to keep a written note of alleged incidents of bullying, so that investigators may check on the veracity of the allegations in respect of time, shifts, place, rota and general opportunity and circumstance.

The existence of a company policy on bullying and a commitment from the top to it often serves due notice on bullies that their behaviour is unacceptable and will result in disciplinary penalty.

Personnel departments must handle any subsequent investigations sensitively and with respect for both parties. Line managers should always be receptive and sympathetic.

Case Study

The Trustee Savings Bank has a specific policy on bullying and has produced a guidance document for staff. It states:

No form of harassment should be tolerated. It should not be accepted as a fact of working life. Bullying and victimisation can also be forms of harassment. Bullying is where an individual abuses a position of power and authority over another person.

Examples of this are:

- continually shouting at, or humiliating, an individual in front of their colleagues

- picking on one person where there is a common problem

- frightening an individual with physical threats.

The TSB policy contains a procedure for dealing with complaints. It recommends employees keep a written record of any incidents and deal with the problems informally at first.

In 1996, research by the Institute of Personnel & Development found that one in eight employees had been bullied in the past five years and more than half said that bullying was commonplace in their organisations.

In December 1996, a solicitor's clerk succeeded in a private prosecution against his former employer for bullying him. He was sworn at and assaulted by one of the firm's solicitors. He was awarded £30 compensation and £785 costs by the magistrates' court, who convicted the defendant after the Crown Prosecution Service had declined to bring charges.

Janice Thomas, an office manager in a pallet company who had to wear ear defenders to protect herself from the obscene language of her boss and senior managers who swore constantly, was awarded £1780 compensation by an industrial tribunal for unfair constructive dismissal in 1996.

Summary

- Harassment covers a range of behaviour which is unwanted and is offensive to the recipient. This can include both sexual and racial harassment.

- In 1996, 65% of organisations in the private sector operated a sexual harassment policy, up from 20% in 1992.

- Harassment at work is widespread and has damaging effects on both the individual concerned and the organisation.

- Besides requiring an employer to take action against a harasser, the victim can also sue through the courts for compensation.

- A policy, once devised, should be effectively communicated to all staff and training provided for managers, supervisors and designated officers.

- An employer may be held responsible for e-mail harassment carried out on company premises or with company equipment.

- Employers are under both a legal and moral duty to ensure that their employees do not have to suffer the indignity and humiliation of harassment.

- It is no defence in cases of harassment for employees to say "it was only a joke".

- Procedures laid out in a harassment policy should explain to whom a complaint can be made, the scope of investigations and the time limits involved.

- Bullying at work involves intentional intimidation or belittling of an individual, usually by a person who has power over them. It is likely to cause loss of morale, increased absenteeism and poor productivity among victims.

Useful Reading

Racial Harassment at Work is available from:

Commission for Racial Equality
Elliot House
10–12 Arlington Street
London SW1E 5EH
Tel: 0171-828 7022

Sexual Harassment in the Workplace (PL923) and *Racial Harassment in the Workplace* (PL924) are available from:

Department for Education and Employment
ISCO 5
The Paddock
Frizinghall
Bradford BF9 4HD

Sex Discrimination Decisions No. 16 — Sexual Harassment is available from:
Equal Opportunities Commission
Overseas House
Quay Street
Manchester M3 3HN
Tel: 0161-833 9244

Adams, A, *Bullying at Work, how to confront and overcome it.*
Virago, ISBN 1 85 381 542 X

TSB Guidance on Bullying is available from:
BIFU Equal Opportunities Department
Sheffield House
1b Amity Grove
Raynes Park
London SW20 OLG
Tel: 0181-946 9151

Dealing with harassment and bullying at work: information pack
is available from:
Gloucester City Council
Department of Human Resources
Herbert Warehouse
The Docks
Gloucester GL1 2EQ
Tel: 01452 522232

Bullying at Work (HS1496) is available from:
Unison
1 Mabledon Place
London WC1H 9AJ

3 Religion

Introduction

The UK is a multi-faith and multicultural society in which many different religions are likely to be represented in the workplace. Respecting another's religious beliefs is important from a human rights standpoint as well as from a business and legal perspective.

Under Article 9 of the **European Convention on Human Rights**:

> *Everyone has the right to freedom of thought, conscience and religion; this right includes freedom to change his religion or belief, and freedom, either alone or in community with others and in public or private, to manifest his religion or belief in worship, teaching, practice and observance.*

Freedom to manifest one's religion or beliefs shall be subject only to such limitations as are prescribed by law and are necessary in a democratic society, in the interests of public safety, for the protection of public order, health or morals, or for the protection of the rights and freedoms of others.

The Court of Human Rights may declare that an individual's rights have been violated under the convention but this does not of itself overturn any existing laws or judicial decisions reached within the UK.

The Commission for Racial Equality *Code of Practice for the Elimination of Racial Discrimination and the Promotion of Equality of Opportunity in Employment*, while not law, can be referred to by tribunals, and should be followed by employers. Under the heading "Cultural and Religious Needs" paragraph 1.24 states:

> *Where employees have particular cultural and religious needs which conflict with existing work requirements, it is*

*recommended that employers should consider whether it is
reasonably practicable to vary or adapt these requirements
to enable such needs to be met. For example, it is
recommended that they should not refuse employment to a
turbaned Sikh because he could not comply with
unjustifiable uniform requirements. Other examples of such
needs are:*

(a) observance of prayer times and religious holidays

*(b) wearing of dress such as sarees and the trousers worn
by Asian women.*

Legislation

There is no legislation in England, Wales and Scotland which
specifically outlaws discrimination against a person on the
grounds of his or her religious beliefs. Any claims by
employees must therefore be dealt with under existing
legislation.

In Northern Ireland, the **Fair Employment (Northern
Ireland) Act 1976** and **1989** make it unlawful to discriminate
directly or indirectly against people in employment on
grounds of religious belief or political opinion.

The **Race Relations Act 1976** (RRA) outlaws less
favourable treatment on "racial grounds". Under s.3(1) of
the RRA "racial grounds" are defined as grounds relating to
colour, race, nationality or ethnic or national origins.
Although there is no specific mention of "religion" within
the statutory definition, discrimination on religious grounds
may in certain situations be included within the definition of
"ethnic origin" and thereby provide a complainant with a
remedy.

Racial Groups

Protection for a member of a *religious group* under the RRA
depends on whether that group can be classified as an *ethnic
group*. Ethnicity has a wider connotation than nationality or

race and can include religious and cultural differences as well as purely racial ones.

In *Mandla v Lee* [1983] IRLR 209, the House of Lords held that Sikhs constituted an ethnic group and were thereby covered by the RRA. In the course of the judgment, the court laid down the following essential characteristics of a racial group:

- a long, shared history, of which the group is conscious and which distinguishes it from other groups, and the memory of which it keeps alive
- a cultural tradition of its own, including family and social customs and manners, often associated with religious observance.

In addition, the court also identified other relevant characteristics, which although not essential, one or more of which would commonly be found by the group:

- either a common geographical origin or descent from a small number of common ancestors
- a common language, not necessarily peculiar to that group
- a common literature peculiar to that group
- a common religion different from that of the neighbouring groups or from the general community surrounding it
- a sense of being a minority or being an oppressed or dominant group within a larger community.

In *Mandla*, it was held that a person could be within a protected group whether by birth, or by conversion and adherence.

The criteria established in *Mandla* have since been applied in *Seide v Gillette Industries* [1980] IRLR 427 to include Jews, who were held by the EAT to be both a religious and an ethnic group.

In *Dawkins v Department of Environment* [1993] ICR 517, the Court of Appeal held that Rastafarians were not to be regarded as an ethnic group. The case arose because

Dawkins, a Rastafarian, refused to cut his dreadlocks and was thus refused a job as a driver. The court held that Rastafarians did not have a separate identity based on their ethnic origins and neither did they have a long shared history. They were, in effect, a religious sect.

Muslims were held not to be members of an ethnic group in *Nyazi v Rymans Ltd* (EAT 6/88), in which an employee was refused leave by her employer for a muslim festival and similarly, in *Commission for Racial Equality v Precision Manufacturing Services Ltd* (COIT 4106/91), in which an employer was alleged to have instructed the local Jobcentre not to send him any muslims as job applicants. The muslim faith covered numerous nations, languages and colours, their only common denominator being religion and religious culture.

A key determinant in whether a religious group will be within the statutory definition of a racial group is whether the group in question has developed historically through influence and conversion as opposed to migration. If it has, it is less likely to be able to gain protection under the RRA's definition of ethnic origin.

Direct and Indirect Discrimination

Unlawful discrimination within the RRA can be either direct or indirect. Direct discrimination arises where an individual suffers less favourable treatment on racial grounds which he or she would not have suffered but for his or her racial origin, nationality, national origins or colour.

Indirect discrimination arises if four conditions are fulfilled.

1. A requirement or condition is applied across the board.
2. The proportion of members of the complainant's racial group which can comply with it is considerably smaller than the proportion of those outside the racial group who can comply.

3. The requirement or condition cannot be shown to be *justifiable*.

4. It is to the detriment of the complainant because he or she cannot comply.

Requirements or conditions could involve dress or appearance rules or being available for work at certain times of the day or week.

It was stated by the Court of Appeal in *Hampson v Department of Education and Science* [1989] ICR 179, that when considering the defence of "justification", a balancing exercise has to be undertaken comparing the discriminatory effects of the requirement or condition and the reasonable needs of the employer's business.

In *Board of Governors of St. Mathias Church of England School v Crizzle* [1993] IRLR 472, the EAT held that it was justifiable for the employers to insist that applicants for the post of headteacher be "committed communicant Christians". Crizzle, the deputy head at the school, who was a woman of Asian origin and a non-communicant Roman Catholic, was rejected for the post. It was held that the school's objective of having a headteacher who could lead the school in spiritual worship and would foster the Anglo-Catholic ethos of the school, was legitimate and reasonable. The imposition of the requirement in order to achieve the objective was reasonable and having balanced the discriminatory effect on the applicant's racial group as against the reasonable needs of the school, the objective was justifiable.

In *Wetstein v Misprestige Management Services Ltd* (EAT 523/91), a jewish employee who was required to work after sunset on Fridays failed in her claim of indirect race discrimination because she couldn't show that a considerably smaller proportion of Jews would not be able to comply with the requirement compared to the number of non-Jews who could do so. This was based on the fact that only between 5%–10% of Jews were strict observers of the Sabbath.

An industrial tribunal in *Hoffman v Marks and Spencer plc* (COIT 109/95) found it justifiable for the company to reject a jewish applicant for the post of food technologist because she was unwilling to eat the full range of foods which were likely to be given to her so she could test them. Although the requirement to be able to eat all foods had a disproportionate impact on Jews, it was nevertheless justifiable on non-racial grounds and the requirement fell squarely within the employer's reasonable needs.

Dismissal

Sometimes an employer dismisses an employee whose behaviour is considered inappropriate in a religious setting.

In *Gibbons v Governors of St. Peters Roman Catholic Junior School* (COIT 25816/96), an industrial tribunal heard that a Roman Catholic teacher had been dismissed for explaining the act of suicide. She was reading a story from a children's book to her class of 10 and 11 year olds in which one of the characters had committed suicide. The teacher was asked how that would have been done and she replied: "probably by putting a revolver in their mouth and shooting themselves". Although it was a matter of professional judgment as to how the teacher should have answered the pupils' questions on such a matter, her approach could not be viewed as being in conflict with the teaching of the Catholic Church or in any way as encouraging or excusing suicide. The tribunal held that she had been unfairly dismissed.

In *O'Neill v Governors of St. Thomas More RCVA Upper School* [1996] IRLR 372, a teacher of religious education and personal relationships was dismissed after it became known that she had become pregnant as a result of a relationship with a Roman Catholic Priest known in the locality and at the school where he was a regular visitor. Mrs O'Neill was not permitted to return to the school after her maternity leave and she resigned. The Governors said that her position within the school as a religious education teacher, having had a relationship with a Catholic Priest, was untenable. The EAT held that she had been unfairly dismissed on the basis of her *pregnancy*. The other factors surrounding the Governors' actions — the paternity of the child, the publicity her situation had generated, and the untenability of her position as a religious education teacher at the school — were all causally related to the fact that she was pregnant.

In *Clarke v Greater Manchester Scientific Services* (1996) (unreported), a Roman Catholic environmental chemist lost his unfair dismissal claim after he was sacked for refusing to test samples from hospital incinerators because they might have been used to destroy aborted foetuses and this had conflicted with his religious beliefs.

Clothing and Appearance

Potential difficulties can arise where an employer insists that staff wear a particular uniform or comply with a stated dress and appearance code. For instance, Sikhs are required to grow their hair and wear turbans. Muslim women must dress in a conservative and modest way so as to conceal their shape and cannot reveal their arms and legs.

An employer should be sensitive to the religious views of staff and should try to accommodate them if at all possible. It may in fact be very difficult for an employer to be able to justify the need for all staff to wear a prescribed uniform.

In *Malik v Bertram Personnel Group Ltd* (COIT 4343\90), a female muslim was rejected from a job because she refused, on religious grounds, to wear a skirt which was part of the company's uniform. The requirement to do so discriminated against women in the local Pakistani community, most of whom were muslim. The claim that the requirement was justified in order to project a corporate image was rejected. It would also have been feasible for the employers to allow muslim women to wear trousers under their company overalls and still present a good image to customers.

Orthodox Jews can come into conflict with employers' dress codes (the strict requirement to keep their heads covered; some Orthodox Jewish sects only wear black clothes). In such situations an employer might allow some leeway and permit exceptions to the general dress code where an employee has a genuinely held religious conviction.

A requirement that staff be clean-shaven or have short hair can be justified on hygiene and/or health and safety grounds but it is for the employer to demonstrate the connection. In *Singh v Rowntree Mackintosh Ltd* [1979] IRLR 199 and *Panesar v The Nestlé Company Ltd* [1980] IRLR 64, it was held to be a justifiable requirement for an employer to refuse to employ staff with beards for hygiene reasons, even though this discriminated against Sikhs. An employer must, however, consider whether hygiene can be maintained by providing appropriate protective clothing (beard snoods).

Note that health and safety factors take priority over religious beliefs when it comes to wearing protective equipment.

Male Sikhs were given a special concession under s.11 of the **Employment Act 1989**, in that they do not have to wear safety helmets on construction sites because they wear turbans. "Construction sites" are defined as "any place where any building, operations or works of engineering construction are being undertaken". At places other than construction sites (for example a steel mill as in *Dhanjal v British Steel General Steels* (COIT 2692/119)), it can be justifiable for an employer to insist that a Sikh wears a safety helmet in a hard hat area.

Praying During Working Hours

Certain faiths such as Islam, require their followers to pray during the course of each day and this can obviously impinge on working time. Muslims, for instance, are called to prayer five times each day: at dawn, early afternoon, late afternoon, sunset and at night. The prayers necessitate a state of cleanliness which requires the ritual washing under running water of the face, hands, forearms and feet. This may also be achieved by a bath or shower. The prayers themselves take between 10 and 20 minutes and can be undertaken alone or in groups. If it is not practical to go to an established Mosque, then prayer can be offered in any clean place, for instance in specially prepared room on company premises.

The timing of the prayers can normally be made to coincide with an employee's work breaks but on Friday muslims are required to worship at mid-day in a communal setting wherever possible. In *Ahmad v Inner London Education Authority* [1978] 1 All ER 574, it was held that a muslim employee who was employed as a teacher did not have the right to take time off in breach of his contract to attend communal prayer at his mosque on Fridays. This would have caused an unacceptable disruption to the school timetable.

For Jews, the Sabbath begins one and a quarter hours before nightfall on Fridays, after which no work can be done, and during the winter months when sunset is earlier, this can conflict with work commitments. However, according to the Jewish Board of Deputies, leaving work early to observe the sabbath only requires Jews to make up an average of 1.8% of a working week.

Jewish employees have no protection under the law to prevent their contracts of employment requiring them to work on Saturdays and a refusal to work on their Sabbath can ultimately result in their fair dismissal. However, an employer should not insist on it unless there are compelling operational reasons demanding it.

Time off for Religious Festivals

The terms of an individual's contract of employment, whether express or implied by custom, are important in determining any entitlement to take time off to celebrate religious festivals or attend other high holy days.

Non-Christian religious festivals may not coincide with employers' shut-down periods or they may not be convenient times for staff absence. An employer must strike a balance between legitimate business needs and the religious and cultural needs of a diverse workforce. Where possible, an employer should try to accommodate requests for time off for religious festivals and this may be allowed on the basis of unpaid holiday or as part of their annual paid leave.

In *JH Walker Ltd v Hussain & others* [1996] IRLR 11, a large number of Asian employees, nearly all of whom were Muslims, were awarded £1000 each in compensation for being disciplined by their employer for taking a day's holiday to celebrate a religious festival, in defiance of a management instruction. They were disciplined despite the fact that they were willing to put in extra time to deal with any backlog of work which might be caused by their absence. The employees' claims of indirect race discrimination were founded on their racial group, all originating from India or Pakistan, and not on the grounds of their religion. The employer was held to have intentionally discriminated against them by the application of the strict rule on holidays because he knew that it would adversely affect muslim employees. The motive of the employer in behaving as he did in applying the rule did not alter the fact that he acted intentionally. The tribunal was entitled to find that, on balance, the rule was not justified.

Orthodox Jews are required to take up to 13 days off work in order to fulfil religious observations. A recent guide for employers has been produced by the Board of Deputies of British Jews and supported by the Commission for Racial

Equality. The guide points out that difficulties can be minimised by careful planning and Jews often volunteer to work on Christian holidays such as Christmas and Easter to compensate for taking religious days off. More usually though, Jewish festivals are taken as part of annual leave.

Religious Knives

Devout Sikhs are required to carry a kirpan (dagger). This protects Sikh dignity and self-respect and represents a readiness to fight in self-defence or in the protection of the weak. In Britain, the majority of Sikhs do not adhere to the requirement, although for those that do, it may be a symbolic knife and concealed upon them. As such, there should be no health and safety considerations in most jobs and it need not conflict with any uniform requirements.

Under the **Criminal Justice and Public Order Act 1988**, it is an offence to have a knife in a public place unless the defendant can prove it was carried for a lawful purpose. A devout Sikh would have a good reason to carry a kirpan dagger provided it was consistent with their religious belief at the time.

Dietary Requirements

Some faiths, such as muslims and Jews, maintain strict dietary codes for their adherents. Where an employer provides food for its employees, it is good policy to offer a range of dishes bearing in mind the beliefs of those to whom it is offered. It is especially important where food in a staff canteen is provided at a subsidised rate because if muslim or jewish workers were unable to eat it for religious reasons, they would be suffering a detriment of less favourable treatment and could claim that they were indirectly discriminated against on racial grounds. Providing an alternative vegetarian dish is one option which avoids serving meat and can have a wide appeal to all the staff.

Northern Ireland

Under the **Fair Employment (Northern Ireland) Act 1976**, it is unlawful to discriminate against a person on the grounds of their religious belief. Public tribunals were set up by the **Fair Employment (Northern Ireland) Act 1989** and unlimited compensation can be awarded to successful claimants.

The aim of the legislation is to reduce less favourable treatment based on religion and to help eliminate workplace sectarianism and intimidation. According to the Fair Employment Commission, more than 10% of people in Northern Ireland have experienced some form of sectarian harassment at work.

In 1996, Shorts Brothers paid £10,000 to a Catholic man who successfully complained that he had to work in a sectarian and intimidating atmosphere when the Fair Employment Tribunal held that he had suffered less favourable treatment on the grounds of his religious and political beliefs.

A Protestant who was refused promotion in favour of a less-qualified Roman Catholic candidate was awarded over £20,000 in *Brown v Department of the Environment* (1996) (unreported). His employers had used a policy of positive discrimination in an attempt to achieve a fairer balance of religious denominations within the Department of the Environment.

In *Croft Inns Ltd v Smyth* [1995] IRLR 84, the Northern Ireland Court of Appeal held that an employer was liable for unlawful discrimination on religious grounds against a Roman Catholic barman because they had failed to respond to a sectarian threat to his safety from a customer and he had resigned as a consequence, believing his life was at risk. He was awarded £12,871 compensation.

In 1996, the Fair Employment Commission issued a set of guidelines for employers to help them deal with sectarian harassment in the workplace.

Summary

- An employer should try, wherever possible, to accommodate the religious and cultural beliefs of employees.

- Rules which discriminate against certain faiths, for example the imposition of a dress code, may not be justifiable, particularly if small variations of the rules could enable them to accommodate the needs of all employees.

- In deciding whether a dismissal was fair, industrial tribunals will take into account the applicant's position, balanced against the business needs of the organisation.

- Prayer time should, where possible, be arranged to coincide with existing work breaks and an employee may not be justified in disrupting the working day in order to pray.

- Where food is provided by employers, say in a subsidised staff canteen, refusing to provide food which meets religious dietary requirements may be viewed as less favourable treatment.

- In Northern Ireland, it is unlawful to discriminate against a person on the grounds of their religious belief.

Useful Reading

Sectarian Harassment at Work: Employer Guidelines is available from:

FEC
Andras House

60 Great Victoria Street
Belfast BT2 7BB

Guide to recruiting Jewish people is available from:
Board of Deputies of British Jews
Tel: 0171-543 5400

4 Alcohol and Drugs in the Workplace

Alcohol

The drinking habits of staff can have significant implications for both the individuals concerned and their employer's business. Dealing with drink-related problems is an important issue in two particular situations. First, where employees themselves have access to alcohol such as in public houses and off-licences. Second, when they work in an environment where the public has free access and therefore they may come into regular contact with people who use and abuse alcohol. Typical examples include staff who work in benefit offices, betting shops and railway stations. In these circumstances there is an increased risk to the health of the employees concerned as a result of alcohol consumption.

Statistics

Although drinking alcohol is essentially a personal matter and part of social life, it can have major workplace implications. The CBI estimates that drink-related absenteeism causes 8 million working days to be lost every year, at a cost of £1.7 billion to the economy. The charity Alcohol Concern estimates that up to 14 million working days are lost annually at a cost of £2 billion.

Other worrying statistics indicate that up to 25% of accidents at work involve intoxicated workers. Recent research by the Institute of Personnel & Development found that one third of organisations they surveyed acknowledged that they have had incidents arising from alcohol abuse. About two thirds of organisations have an alcohol policy.

ACAS and the Department for Education & Employment strongly urge all employers to introduce one.

Apart from being driven by commercial considerations, employers should also consider the health and welfare of the staff they employ. In Britain, a total of 1.3 million men and 500,000 women drink at levels which are harmful to their health and another 7 million, including 13% of all women, exceed the recommended weekly levels, which were raised in December 1995 from 14 units to 21 units per week. Research published in March 1997 by Alcohol Concern found that 1 person in 20 was dependent on alcohol compared with 1 in 45 dependent on drugs such as ecstasy, cannabis, cocaine, heroin, LSD, tranquilisers and sleeping pills. There are up to 33,000 alcohol-related deaths each year and about 28,000 hospital admissions due to alcohol dependence or poisoning. According to a report by the Royal Colleges, alcohol misuse is associated with 60% of suicide attempts, 40% of domestic violence, 15% of deaths from road traffic accidents, 26% of deaths from drowning and 39% of deaths in fires.

Apart from the human and personal cost involved in incidents such as these, an employer has a direct interest in fostering a happy and efficient workforce where staff attend work regularly and in a competent state of health. Permitting staff to drink during the working day and supplying it on the premises, or at business functions, can be exacerbating an existing personal problem for some individual employees.

The Effects of Alcohol

Contrary to popular belief, alcohol is a depressant which slows down the processes occurring in the brain. In other words, it makes you less alert but at the same time, gives you a strong but false sense of confidence. The chances of having an accident are increased when alcohol is consumed because it slows down your reactions, affects your judgment on important matters such as speed and distance, affects your accuracy, performance and co-ordination and can lead you to take greater risks. All these consequences have serious workplace implications.

The body gets rid of alcohol from the bloodstream at a very slow rate, equivalent to half a pint of beer, or one single measure of spirits, per hour. Therefore, it will take up to eight hours to get rid of the alcohol from drinking four pints of beer. If an employee has been drinking over a long period the previous night, they may well be still affected by it at work the next morning. British Rail recently dismissed a signal repair and maintenance worker for arriving at work at 7am when more than double the drink-drive limit. Staff are told not to drink within eight hours of taking up duty and random tests are carried out. In *R v Cook* (1995) (unreported), a station master who arrived for work at Glasgow Central Station was found to be nearly twice the legal alcohol limit for someone having control of trains. Not only was he sacked by his employers, he was also sentenced to 150 hours community service by Glasgow Sheriff Court.

Herein lies one of the problems for employers — how to control the habits of staff in their own free time. Explaining to them the rate of decline of alcohol in the bloodstream would be the first step; impressing on them the adverse effects of arriving at work under the influence and then starting to operate machinery or drive vehicles for example, would be the second step.

Effects or Consequences of Alcohol on Employees at Work

Alcohol consumption can lead to the following repercussions:

- increased absenteeism and sickness rates
- enhanced likelihood of workplace accidents
- reduced productivity and lower quality of work
- strained workplace relationships
- damage to employer's public image.

The Causes of Alcohol Misuse

There are many factors which can contribute to alcohol misuse. Some will arise from the workplace, some from home, and some will be a combination of both. These include:

- the volume of work
- monotonous or boring work
- unsocial or irregular hours
- under or over-promotion
- workplace stress
- access to alcohol at work
- working alone or without supervision
- marital or family problems
- family illness or bereavement
- financial difficulties
- pressure from colleagues or friends.

How to Recognise Employees with a Drink Problem

Apart from certain obvious outward signs of alcohol misuse, the following are possible indicators:

- lateness and absenteeism
- poor work or output
- unreliability
- impaired concentration, memory and judgment
- involvement in accidents.

Employers should investigate incidents or occurrences as they arise, in order to find out the true reason for their cause as they may not be drink-related.

In January 1996, the Chemical Bank issued a policy booklet to staff on substance abuse. It outlines the tell-tale symptoms of abuse and tells employees to report their colleagues. The Trustee Savings Bank has a similar approach and tells employees to inform a manager if they believe a colleague is abusing drink or drugs.

Legal Dimension of Drink in the Workplace

There can be health and safety implications of employees under the influence of alcohol while at work. Employers are under a statutory duty to provide a safe place of work and to engage safe employees who will not constitute a danger to themselves or others.

Drink problems associated with employees can be split into two categories:

(a) staff who drink excessively on one or more occasion but who are not physically or psychologically dependent on alcohol

(b) employees who are alcohol-dependent and whose consistent drinking continually or repeatedly affects their work.

Although the difference in these two categories of drinkers is easily stated, in practice it can be difficult for an employer to distinguish between them. It is important to do so, however, because the correct approach for non-dependent drinkers is to deal with the matter as a *disciplinary* issue, whereas dependent or problem drinkers should be treated from a *capability* perspective.

Misconduct

Where, in the case of non-dependent drinkers, an employer treats an incident as misconduct, the following factors are relevant.

1. The seriousness of the incident. In *Gray Dunn & Company Ltd v Edwards* [1980] IRLR 23, it was held to be fair to dismiss a night shift worker who was under the influence of drink at work and posed a health and safety risk and who thereby endangered his colleagues.

2. Whether the employer has any rules covering alcohol in the workplace and whether those rules have been communicated to all staff, and applied consistently. In *Brooks v Skinner* [1984] IRLR 379, it was held to be unfair dismissal to sack an employee who was in contravention

of a rule stating that anyone who was incapable of returning to work following the Christmas party because of drink, would be summarily dismissed. However, the rule had been agreed only between the employer and the trade union and individual employees had not received personal notice of it.

3. The type of work the employee does. In *Paul v East Surrey District Health Authority* [1995] IRLR 305, a charge nurse at a mental hospital drank whisky while on duty, got aggressive and began abusing and disturbing the patients. Ultimately, he had to be restrained and the police were called. His subsequent dismissal for gross misconduct was held to be fair because he was in dereliction of his duty to care for the patients.

4. Whether the employer condones or encourages drink, perhaps by supplying or paying for it. In *Kelly v Volex Accessories Division* [1988] IRLB 367, it was held to be unfair to dismiss an employee who was under the influence of alcohol following celebrations of his pools win, because the employers had, in the past, tolerated drink on the premises when staff had things to celebrate. In *Whitbread Beer Company v Williams* [1996] IRLB 560, three employees were held by the Court of Appeal to have been unfairly dismissed for drunken conduct following a company behavioural skills course run in one of their employer's hotels because the employers had provided free drink.

5. The example which the employee is setting both inside and outside the company. Even where the staff member's drunken behaviour occurs outside work, this can have an adverse impact on the employer's business where, for instance, the conduct creates bad publicity for the employer. This could arise where the employee is using the employer's company vehicle outside work or is otherwise wearing some company insignia.

At the Royal Liverpool University Hospital, alcohol is forbidden at staff parties and at lunchtime and this is policed by random breath tests. Staff who take time off due to alcohol-related illness do not receive paid sick leave. Employees found with traces of alcohol in their breath face disciplinary procedures and, potentially, dismissal.

Capability

As far as dependent drinkers are concerned, employers need to treat this as they would treat an employee with any other type of illness. In all issues of capability, employers must investigate the matter fully, consult with the employee, get medical feedback and a prognosis.

Employers are under a duty to gain independent medical advice before dismissing, they need to discuss the matter with the employee, consider how best to rehabilitate him or her, take all reasonable steps to establish the true position and decide on a timeframe for the employee's recovery.

Having done all of this, the question is how long should an employer wait for the employee to improve before taking any further action? This depends on a variety of factors.

- Is the employee a key worker?
- Can their job be covered by other staff?
- The size of the business.
- Estimated duration for rehabilitation.
- The attitude/co-operation of the employee being treated.

However, in the final analysis, an employer may ultimately dismiss under the "capability" ground in s.98(2)(a) of the **Employment Rights Act 1996**.

Alcohol Screening

It is becoming increasingly common for employers to insist that successful candidates undergo screening for excessive alcohol use which could affect their work performance. In *Baker v Kaye* [1996] QBD TLR, a television executive had his £45,000 per annum job offer in international sales withdrawn following a medical report which stated that he was not medically fit for employment with the television company

NBC. Although the report did not brand him an alcoholic, he was assessed as a "spree drinker" and thereby likely to drink alcohol excessively while working which would affect the sharpness of his thought processes.

Where an employer wishes to screen existing staff for alcohol, there should be an express contractual term for this. Employees should also be left in no doubt about the consequences of a positive test result and they should be made aware that a failure to submit to a test will constitute a disciplinary offence.

Alcohol Policy Checklist

The following elements should be considered when drawing up a policy on alcohol at work:

- the company's rules on alcohol at work
- a statement that the organisation recognises that an alcohol problem may be an illness to be treated in the same way as any other illness
- a statement that the rules on alcohol at work will apply to any contractors visiting the organisation
- the potential dangers to the health and safety of drinkers and their colleagues if an alcohol problem is untreated
- the importance of early identification and treatment of an alcohol problem
- the help available, eg from managers, supervisors, company doctor, occupational health service or outside agency*
- the disciplinary position, for instance an organisation may agree to suspend disciplinary action in cases of misconduct, where an alcohol problem is a factor, on condition that the employee follows a suitable course of action — where gross misconduct is involved an alcohol problem may be taken into account in determining disciplinary action
- the provision of paid sick leave for agreed treatment

- the individual's right to return to the same job after effective treatment and any conditions that may apply
- an assurance of confidentiality
- whether or not an individual will be allowed a second course of treatment if he or she relapses
- termination of employment on grounds of ill health where treatment is unsuccessful
- a statement that the policy applies to all employees
- a statement that the policy will be kept under regular review to evaluate its effectiveness.

* Employers may also provide counselling to employees through an Employee Assistance Programme.

Drugs

Drug use and abuse is on the increase and is rising faster than alcohol abuse. According to the British Crime Survey, about 3 million people take illegal drugs and 28% of 16–29 year olds were found to be users. In a MORI poll in 1996, 45% of 20–24 year olds said they had experimented with cannabis, and 28% with amphetamines. Body-building drugs, often used in an employer's gym, can also be a problem and there are some 48 illegal anabolic steroids.

A recent survey by the Institute of Personnel & Development found that 15% of companies had received reports that their employees had used illegal drugs and it is acknowledged that 30% of known illicit drug users are in employment. However, only 54% of UK businesses have a policy on drugs.

Research into drug abuse by the International Labour Organisation found that drug use was not limited to any specific occupation but that it was especially prevalent in certain occupations. These included: doctors, nurses, military personnel, business executives, pilots, assembly line workers and long-distance lorry drivers.

Research from the United States has revealed that employees who use drugs are a third less productive than their colleagues, 3.6 times more likely to injure themselves or their co-workers and 2.5 times more likely to be absent from work for 8 days or more.

Effects of Drugs Misuse in the Workplace

The potentially harmful effects of drugs misuse are as follows:

- increased sickness rates and absenteeism levels
- an increased risk of accident
- a deterioration in the quality and quantity of work
- damaged working relationships with work colleagues due to unpredictable and irrational behaviour
- an increased propensity to be involved in criminal activity, both outside and inside the workplace in order to support the drug habit.

All of the above have important implications for an employer.

The Legal Dimensions of Drugs in the Workplace

Under the **Misuse of Drugs Act 1971** (MDA), it is an offence to supply or produce controlled drugs without authority. These include heroin, cocaine, cannabis and amphetamines. An employer clearly needs to prevent the commission of criminal offences on the premises and must take the appropriate action to combat drug dealing among staff.

Simply turning a blind eye to the problem is no solution for an employer because, under the MDA, it is an offence to knowingly allow controlled drugs to be supplied, produced, used or simply held on their premises.

The **Health and Safety at Work, etc Act 1974** places a statutory duty on employers to provide and maintain a safe place of work and a safe system of work together with adequate supervision. Employers must ensure that employees don't injure themselves and others and the likelihood of this increases where drug-taking employees use machinery, equipment or vehicles. Employees themselves have a responsibility for their own and their colleagues' welfare.

The **Control of Substances Hazardous to Health Regulations 1994** also covers substances which, although not necessarily illegal, can be harmful to health if they are misused.

The Signs of Drug Abuse

Employers should consider running training courses for line managers to help them identify possible indicators of drug abuse among staff. Early recognition can enable management to intervene before a problem gets out of hand and enhance the prospects of rehabilitation for the user.

Physical signs:
- tiredness
- shoddy dressing
- loss in weight
- displaying aggressive behaviour
- irritability
- tendency to become confused
- unpredictable behaviour and mood fluctuations.

Performance-based indicators:
- increased sickness absence
- poor timekeeping
- deteriorating staff relationships
- missing deadlines
- unexpected decrease in work quality
- customer/client complaints.

There could also be telling evidence at work such as the discovery of items heavily associated with drug taking, for instance, needles, syringes, paper twists, small mirrors, scorched spoons, straws, tinfoil.

Causes of Drug Taking

Causes of drug taking can be related to factors both inside and outside the workplace and might include:

- pressure from friends and colleagues
- curiosity
- too much or too little work
- lack of management direction and supervision
- unsocial or irregular hours
- monotonous work
- stress, depression or anxiety.

Employer Action

In all probability, an employer will have rules prohibiting the possession of drugs on the premises, the taking of drugs on the premises or being under the influence of drugs while at work. Contravention of these rules will be classed as gross misconduct with the potential for summary dismissal following disciplinary procedures.

For instance, in *Stanton v Atlantic Steam Navigation Company Ltd* (COIT 701/97), it was held to be fair to dismiss a seaman for using cannabis while at sea because of the potential risk to other seamen on board and the placing of the ship's cargo in jeopardy.

Similarly, in *Anderson v Oak Motor Works Ltd* (COIT 1270/153), it was held to be fair to dismiss two employees found smoking cannabis while at work because health and safety had been jeopardised by their intoxicated state. Furthermore, their actions constituted a criminal offence. In such cases, dismissal is likely to be fair providing a full investigation has been undertaken and a fair procedure followed.

However, if an employer has no specific rule regarding drugs, it will not always be fair to dismiss an employee caught possessing soft drugs at work. In *Moyes v Payless DIY* (COIT 1712/242), a self-confessed social drug user admitted the possession of cannabis at work. However, she said it belonged to a friend for whom she had rolled three joints and, as she had never smoked cannabis herself at work and was not distributing it, her dismissal was held to be unfair.

The effect of drug taking on other employees is also a relevant factor. In *Focus DIY Ltd v Nicholson* (EAT 225/94), a senior employee smoked cannabis at an office party in front of other staff, including her subordinates. Apart from anything else, this compromised her authority in the eyes of her staff and she was held to have been fairly dismissed. In *Mathewson v R B Wilson Dental Labs Ltd* (EAT 144/88), an employee was caught in possession of cannabis in his lunch hour. Although it was for his own use, the impact of the incident on younger employees at work led to a loss of trust and confidence in the employee and he was held to have been fairly dismissed.

If an employee is convicted of drug offences in their private life it was held, in *Gunn v British Waterways Board* (EAT 138/81), that an employer could fairly dismiss an employee where it attracted bad publicity for the employer in the local press.

Although it is possible to treat drugs misuse as a disciplinary issue, the aim of an employer should be to encourage employees to seek help and treatment as quickly as possible. If there is a drug dependence, the issue could be treated as one of illness and thus it becomes a matter of capability.

Drugs Policy Checklist

The following items should be considered when drawing up a policy on drug misuse at work.

* The purpose of the policy, for example: "This policy is designed to help protect employees from the dangers of drug misuse and to encourage those with a drugs problem to seek help".

- A statement that the policy applies to everyone in the organisation.
- The company's rules on the use of drugs at work.
- A statement that the organisation recognises that a drugs problem may be an illness to be treated in the same way as any other illness.
- The potential dangers to the health and safety of drug misusers and their colleagues if a drugs problem is untreated.
- The importance of early identification and treatment.
- The help available, eg from managers, supervisors, company doctor, occupational health service or outside agency.
- The disciplinary position, for example an organisation may agree to suspend disciplinary action where drug misuse is a factor, on condition that the employee follows a suitable course of action.
- The provision of paid sick leave for agreed treatment.
- The individual's right to return to the same job after effective treatment or, where this is not advisable, to suitable alternative employment wherever possible.
- An assurance of confidentiality.

Screening for Drugs

An employer may insist on job applicants having a drugs test but an employer has no inherent right to test existing staff unless the power is reserved in their contracts of employment. In September 1995, the Chief Constable of Grampian Region urged all employers to test their staff for drugs and to insist on an ongoing policy of random testing. In 1996, this was introduced into Grampian Police itself. A growing number of employers conduct random drugs tests on their staff in order to discourage drugs use. In September 1996, two North Sea helicopter companies, Bristow and Bond, introduced random drink and drugs tests for their staff. This was prompted when they both tendered for contracts with Exxon, which stipulated that only companies with such policies were allowed to transport workers to its oil rigs. All applicants for British Rail jobs are screened for drugs and 2.6% fail the test. Similar procedures apply at Shell UK and Texaco. Shell report that about 1% of prospective employees and contractors test drugs positive.

Drugs testing is especially relevant in safety-critical jobs such as transport. Under the **Transport at Work Act 1992**, employers must exercise due diligence to ensure that the performance of staff is not impaired through drink or drugs. At British Rail, testing is also done on relevant staff following an accident or where a member of staff behaves in a suspicious manner. Where safety is paramount, employees owe a duty to the public, their colleagues and to themselves.

Lloyds Register maintains a drugs and drink screening programme for shipping companies, with urine samples providing the basis for testing. Some independent companies provide testing facilities for clients and these are likely to increase in popularity.

In *Sutherland v Sonat Offshore Ltd* (EAT 186/93), a control room operator on an offshore oil rig was held to have been fairly dismissed after he tested positive for cannabis, the results of which he did not challenge.

Note that the **Disability Discrimination Act 1995** specifically excludes drug and alcohol dependence from the definition of disability.

Summary

- Alcohol consumption can have major implications for employers in terms of absenteeism, health, accident rates and productivity.

- Those who indulge in heavy drinking during the evening may still have a high blood alcohol level at work the next morning.

- Employers should investigate employees who are showing symptoms of a drink-related problem.

- It is important to differentiate between non-dependent drinkers and dependent, or problem, drinkers.

- Steps should be taken to help a problem drinker improve. Such a problem may constitute an illness.

- Drugs misuse is rising faster than alcohol misuse.

- It is a criminal offence for an employer knowingly to allow controlled drugs to be kept, supplied or produced on their premises.

- Early recognition of drug abuse can enhance the prospects of rehabilitation. The aim should be to encourage employees to seek help and treatment as quickly as possible.

- An employee convicted of drug or alcohol offences in their private life may still be fairly dismissed if the case has attracted bad publicity for the employer in the press.

- An employer may insist on job applicants having drugs or alcohol tests but has no inherent right to test existing staff unless the power to do so is reserved in their contracts of employment.

Useful Reading

Drug Misuse and the Workplace (PL880) and *Alcohol in the Workplace* (PL859) are available from:

Department for Education and Employment
Cambertown Ltd
Unit 8
Goldthorpe Industrial Estate
Goldthorpe

Rotherham S63 9BL
Tel: 01709 888688

Drugs and Solvents — Things you should know and *Drugs — A parent's guide* are available from:
BAPS
Health Publications Unit
DSS Distribution Centre
Heywood Stores
Manchester Road
Heywood
Lancashire OL10 2PZ
Tel: 0800 555777

Drug Abuse at Work. An HSE Guide for Employers is available from:
PO Box 1999
Sudbury
Suffolk CO10 6FS
Tel: 01787 881165

Health and Employment, ISBN 0 906073 45 6 is available from:
Advisory, Conciliation and Arbitration Service
Head Office
Brandon House
180 Borough High Street
London SE1 1LW
Tel: 0171-210 3000

5   HIV/AIDS

Introduction

According to figures up to December 1996, 28,447 people in
Britain are known to be infected with HIV and since
reporting began in 1982, a total of 13,720 people have
developed AIDS, of whom 9,678 have died. About 2,000 new
cases are confirmed every year, although there may be
currently as many as 150,000 undiagnosed cases of
HIV-positive people in the UK. About 19% of HIV cases in
Britain are thought to have been contracted through
heterosexual contact. In worldwide terms, the total of AIDS
and HIV sufferers had reached 22.6 million by the end of
1996. For employers, there are a range of issues to consider,
including discrimination on recruitment, the way
HIV-positive people are treated at work and their long-term
job security.

What are HIV and AIDS?

AIDS (Acquired Immune Deficiency Syndrome) is a
condition caused by HIV (Human Immunodeficiency Virus).
This virus invades the cells in the body's immune system
that would normally destroy infective organisms such as
viruses and bacteria. As a result, the body's defence system
cannot fight certain infections of the lungs, digestive system,
central nervous system and skin. HIV, the virus which causes
AIDS, survives in body fluids such as blood and semen.
Although the virus has been found in saliva and tears, there
is no documented evidence of the spread of HIV infection
from these secretions.

AIDS is unusual in that it has a very long incubation
period, the average length of time being seven years. During

this period, individuals will be completely well mostly and unaware that they are infected. AIDS is only diagnosed when the immune system is so damaged by the virus that the sufferer becomes susceptible to a range of infections and also to certain types of cancer. During episodes of severe infection the patient will need in-patient hospital care but for the rest of the time the patient will be able to continue life in the community. AIDS proves fatal usually within two years, although medication can sometimes extend this period.

How is the HIV infection spread?

There are many myths and much ill-informed prejudice surrounding HIV and AIDS. The HIV virus is transmitted principally by:
- sexual intercourse with an infected person, male or female
- the sharing of contaminated needles and syringes among injecting drug misusers
- the transfusion of infected blood and blood products
- from an infected mother to her infant before, during, or after birth.

In the working environment, the virus cannot be spread by normal social and work contact between colleagues, such as through airborne droplets from coughing or sneezing, using the same crockery, cutlery, telephones and shared washing and toilet facilities or living in the same accommodation. Only where employees come into close contact with infected blood, semen or other body fluids is there a possibility of infection, possibly through a cut or accidental injection. Certain workers such as doctors, nurses, dentists, laboratory and hospital support staff therefore need to guard against this slight risk. Similarly, emergency service employees, or refuse collectors who may inadvertently get pricked when handling used syringes. Protective equipment should be issued to such people, together with specialised training. The same considerations apply to workplace first-aiders, although again, there have been no recorded cases of infection being transmitted by giving mouth-to-mouth resuscitation.

There have been only two suspected incidents worldwide of health workers passing HIV to patients. In March 1997, two doctors employed in English hospitals and who were involved in gynaecological and obstetric care were found to be HIV-positive. As a consequence, a number of their patients were written to but the risk of infection to them was described as "remote" and there was said to be no risk to any babies.

In *A & Others v Tameside & Glossop Health Authority & Another* [1996] TLR 27 November 1996, it was held that a health authority, finding one of its health workers to be HIV-positive and deciding to inform certain patients of the very remote risk of their having been infected, was not in breach of its duty of care to those patients by informing most of them of that risk by letter. This was held not to be negligent even though it was accepted that the best way of avoiding the risk of causing shock, distress or physical injury to patients was for the Health Authority to supply the information face to face by a suitably qualified person.

Testing/Screening

Employees cannot be compelled to take AIDS tests unless their contracts specify this and it would be necessary in only a minority of jobs, such as health workers. Generally, individuals who become infected are under no duty to inform their employers and may remain fit to work for many years. In this respect, they should be treated like any other employee suffering from a long-term progressive illness. Where disclosure is made to the employer, this information should be treated in full confidence.

Employers Policies on AIDS

According to recent research by the Labour Research Department, over half of public sector employers, but only 16% of private sector employers, have a policy on HIV or AIDS. Having a clear policy on AIDS in the workplace not only helps organisations treat their staff fairly but it also makes good business sense.

ACAS advises all organisations to develop a policy on AIDS and recommends that policies should be developed in conjunction with an education programme and following consultation with employees and their representatives.

Although policies will vary according to the nature of the organisation, there is a minimum standard.

ACAS recommends:

- a brief description of AIDS and how HIV is transmitted
- the organisation's position on screening for HIV infection
- an assurance of confidentiality
- a statement that people with AIDS whose performance suffers or are absent because of AIDS will be treated in the same way as individuals with any other serious illness
- a statement that employees are expected to work normally with a colleague who has or is suspected of having AIDS
- a statement that individuals who refuse to work normally with people with AIDS or who are HIV-positive, will be interviewed to find out the circumstances of their refusal and, if appropriate, dealt with under the organisation's disciplinary procedure
- the help available inside and outside the organisation
- procedures for first aid
- arrangements for staff who travel overseas.

The National AIDS Trust Charter "Companies act!" was launched in 1992 and has attracted 50 signatories. Among its policy guidelines for signatories are:

- addressing HIV and AIDS as separate conditions

- treating AIDS in the same way as any other progressive or debilitating illness
- the employer's policy must make clear by outlining or referring to discipline and grievance procedures what action will be taken if staff breach the terms laid down
- offering redeployment, retraining, flexible working and compassionate leave for carers and those who are HIV-positive.

Confidentiality

Employers owe their staff a duty of mutual trust and confidence. One consequence of this implied contractual term is that an employer should not give any confidential information about an employee to anyone else without his or her consent. Medical information should always be kept confidential. An employer who disclosed the fact that an individual was HIV-positive, or was an AIDS sufferer, could be sued for breach of contract and the employee in question might also resign and claim constructive dismissal.

HIV is not a notifiable illness within the **Public Health (Infectious Diseases) Regulations 1985,** nor are employees under a duty to tell their employer that they are HIV-positive unless their employment contract says so, or there is a requirement in their professional code of conduct, as with nurses.

Pre-employment Screening and Testing of Employees

It is legitimate for an employer to enquire into a job applicant's state of health and to require him or her to undergo medical examinations and blood tests. If an applicant is asked whether he or she is HIV-positive and he or she lies in order to deceive the employer, this may result in him or her being disciplined or dismissed for misrepresentation at a later date. Such a dismissal may be held to be fair but this is not automatic.

A general medical or health check would not normally include an HIV test and an individual must give his or her consent to the test. Under s.3(1) of the **Access to Medical Reports Act 1988**, an employer may not apply to a medical practitioner for the medical report without the employee's consent. This would not apply to a report obtained from a company doctor following an examination specifically undertaken for a particular purpose. Under the **Access to Medical Records Act 1990**, individuals are allowed to have access to health records held about them by any health professional.

Under Article 8 of the **European Convention on Human Rights**, everyone has the right to keep their state of health secret. In *X v Commission of the European Communities* [1995] IRLR 320, it was held by the European Court of Justice (ECJ) that an applicant for a job has the legitimate right to refuse to undergo an HIV test or, indeed, any medical test, and such a refusal must be respected. However, as the ECJ pointed out, an employer has a legitimate interest in pre-recruitment medical examinations and "if the person concerned, after being properly informed, withholds his consent to a test which the medical officer considers necessary in order to evaluate his suitability for the post for which he has applied" (the employer) "cannot be obliged to take the risk of recruiting him".

Although there is nothing unlawful in requiring job applicants to undergo blood tests for HIV, an HIV test is of limited value because it cannot confirm that the person being tested was not infected with the virus in the recent past. This is because it can take up to three months from the time of the infection for antibodies to show up in a blood test. So an individual whose test is negative might, in fact, be infected with the virus. Furthermore, a negative result does not mean that an individual cannot become infected in the future.

An employer may insist on an HIV test as a condition of admitting an employee to the company's life insurance or pension scheme, without this prejudicing his or her future employment.

It is possible to argue that an employer's ban on HIV infected/AIDS applicants constitutes indirect sex discrimination since the ban would have a greater impact on men than women. Similarly, a blanket ban on employing people from certain countries in the world where the infection is prominent could amount to indirect race discrimination.

Employees Working Abroad or Travelling Overseas

Employers are under a duty to warn staff who have to travel abroad or work overseas of the risk involved when visiting countries where hygiene standards may be low, or where blood screening may be inadequate.

Practical advice should be offered and the CBI and the London School of Hygiene and Tropical Medicine can help in this respect. Employees being sent overseas to work could also be given a copy of "The Traveller's Guide to Health" available free from Post Offices.

Some countries, such as Saudi Arabia and Japan, test long-term visitors for HIV. Employers should contact Embassies and High Commissions in London to establish this and, if a test is required, this should be obtained in the UK before the employee goes abroad.

Dealing with Colleagues' Responses to AIDS

Even where an employer has an HIV or AIDS policy, and has provided information for staff, it is still possible that certain employees will harass colleagues whom they either think, or know, are HIV-positive. Employers owe a duty to staff to provide them with a safe place of work and this is compromised where a stressful working environment exists as a consequence of isolated or continuing acts of harassment. All staff should be made aware of the fact that such behaviour is unacceptable and constitutes gross misconduct. It should also be pointed out that it amounts to a breach of their contracts of employment.

In some cases, an employer can come under pressure to sack an infected employee, or certain staff might simply refuse to work with such an individual. In these situations an employer must proceed carefully. The general rule is illustrated in *Philpott v North Lambeth Law Centre* (COIT 11212/86) in which it was held that it was fair to dismiss two employees who refused to work with a newly-appointed colleague whom they claimed would introduce AIDS into the workplace and thereby infect them. In contrast, in *Cormack v TNT Sealion Ltd* (COIT 1825/126) it was held to be fair to dismiss an employee for redundancy on the basis of the suspicions of his colleagues that he was HIV-positive. However, in this case there were special circumstances in that the employee was a chef on an oil rig and the crew lived in close proximity to each other. It was important for there to be a satisfactory working relationship between staff. Therefore, the employer was entitled to take into account the ability of the employee to get on with his fellow workers in the context of a redundancy dismissal.

In *Buck v Letchworth Palace* [1987] IRLB 355, a homosexual cinema projectionist was convicted for soliciting. Two of his colleagues, also projectionists, refused to work alongside him because of their fear of catching AIDS. Even though the employer had made no proper attempt to allay their fears and educate the staff as to the nature of the illness, the industrial tribunal upheld the dismissal of the homosexual projectionist. The employer was deemed to have acted reasonably in responding to the employees' fears. Note, however, that the employee appealed against the decision

and an out-of-court settlement was subsequently reached
between the parties.

Responding to a Client's or Customer's Objections

If a customer or client of the employer discovers that an
employee is infected with the virus, pressure may be put on
the employer to dismiss the employee. In the past, this has
occurred most commonly in the catering or food processing
industries. In fact, HIV cannot be transmitted during food
handling but the perception that it can be is still a strong one
and this can have serious business and market implications
for an employer and its customers or clients.

The first step is for the employer to try to allay the
customer's fears and dispel any prejudices but, if this fails,
consideration should be given to moving the employee to
another job within the organisation. If this is not possible,
dismissal could be a last resort. Even then, it might be
possible for an employee to claim discrimination under the
Disability Discrimination Act 1995.

Dismissal for HIV/AIDS

Testing positive or having AIDS are not, in themselves,
sufficient grounds for dismissing an employee. It will only
be fair to dismiss an AIDS sufferer if his or her illness makes
him or her unfit for work and the employer has undertaken
a fair procedure and followed the general principles
governing serious ill-health dismissals.

An employer must therefore have ascertained the
employee's true medical condition and obtained a
prognosis, maintained full consultation with the employee
throughout and considered suitable alternative employment.

Provided an employer follows the above steps and
follows a fair procedure, a dismissal for ill-health or sickness

absence is likely to be fair under the "capability" ground in s.98(3) of the **Employment Rights Act 1996** (ERA). It might also be possible to argue that the contract of employment has been frustrated at common law. In the limited circumstances where an employee can be shown to be a health risk to others, dismissal could be fair for "some other substantial reason" under s.98(1)(b) of the ERA.

Disability Discrimination Act 1995

Under the **Disability Discrimination Act 1995** (DDA), the HIV infection is classified as a "progressively disabling condition". Companies with 20 or more employees are now under a duty to make "reasonable adjustments" to working conditions, hours and equipment in order to overcome the practical effects of a disability. Note that the DDA does not prevent discrimination against someone who is HIV-positive but asymptomatic and is therefore outwardly healthy. Once such individuals develop certain symptoms of AIDS or are diagnosed as suffering from AIDS however, they will be protected under the Act.

Under the DDA, an individual has the right not to receive "less favourable treatment" on the grounds of his or her disability. The right not to be discriminated against applies to recruitment, promotion, training, terms and conditions of employment and termination. Less favourable treatment of a disabled person in the employment context will be an act of unlawful discrimination unless the employer, or prospective employer, can justify it. In order to achieve this, a justification has to be both material to the circumstances of the particular case and "substantial".

It is arguable that an employer who gives way to outside pressure to dismiss an infected employee will not be able to justify the dismissal under the DDA in that the reason will not be held to be sufficiently "substantial" within the Act. This remains to be seen.

In the context of AIDS, an employer must not treat an employee less favourably, when dismissing through incapability, than it would any other employee suffering from any other terminal illness.

A successful claim under the DDA can result in an award of unlimited damages by an industrial tribunal.

Summary

- Employers must consider a range of issues concerning AIDS and HIV infection affecting recruitment, discrimination, treatment at work and long-term job security.

- In the working environment, the virus cannot be spread by normal social and work contact between colleagues.

- Employees cannot be compelled to take AIDS tests unless their contracts specify this and, generally, individuals who become infected are under no duty to inform their employers.

- Employees who are infected with HIV/AIDS should be treated like any other employee suffering from a long-term progressive illness.

- More than half of public sector employers, and 16% of private sector employers, have a policy on HIV or AIDS.

- Employees' medical information must be kept confidential. An employer who disclosed the fact that an individual was HIV-positive, or was an AIDS sufferer, could be sued for breach of confidence.

- When recruiting, it is legitimate for an employer to enquire into a job applicant's state of health but an individual must give consent for an HIV test and has the right to refuse.

- Employers must warn staff who have to travel, or work, abroad of the risks involved in visiting countries where the infection may be prevalent or blood screening inadequate. In addition, some countries require long-term visitors to undertake tests.

- Employers must take steps to discipline staff who harass colleagues whom they either think or know are HIV-positive.

- If a client or customer complains about an employee who is infected with the virus, steps should be taken to allay their fears before more serious action, such as moving the employee to another job, is taken.

- An individual diagnosed as suffering from AIDS is protected under the **Disability Discrimination Act 1995** and has the right not to receive "less favourable treatment" on the grounds of their disability.

Useful Reading

Employment Booklet: a guide about rights at work for people affected by HIV and AIDS is available from:
The Terrence Higgins Trust
52–54 Gray's Inn Road
London WC1X 8JU
Tel: 0171-831 0330

AIDS and Employment (PL811) and *AIDS and Work — The Facts Employees should know* (PL917) are available from:
Department for Education and Employment
Cambertown Ltd
Unit 8

Goldthorpe Industrial Estate
Goldthorpe
Rotherham S63 9BL
Tel: 01709 888688

HIV, AIDS and the workplace is available from:
Labour Research Department
78 Blackfriars Road
London SE1 8HF
Tel: 0171-928 3649

Working with AIDS: a guide for business and business people and
Complete HIV Manager are available from:
Employers' Advisory Service on AIDS and HIV
PO Box HP346
Leeds LS6 1UL
Tel: 0113 294 1212

*Employment and AIDS: a review of the Companies act! business
charter on HIV and AIDS* and *The Statement of Employment
Principles for HIV and AIDS* are available from:
National AIDS Trust
New City Cloisters
188–196 Old Street
London EC1V 9FR
Tel: 0171-814 6767

6   Stress

What is Stress?

According to the Health and Safety Executive, stress is defined as:

> ...*the reaction people have to excessive pressures or other types of demand placed on them. It arises when they worry that they can't cope.*

Stress can involve physical effects, including:

- increased heart rate
- increased sweating
- headaches
- dizziness
- blurred vision
- aching neck and shoulders
- skin rashes
- a lowering of resistance to infection.

Stress can also have behavioural effects, such as:

- increased anxiety and irritability
- a tendency to drink and smoke more
- difficulty in sleeping
- poor concentration
- loss of interest and motivation
- an inability to deal calmly with everyday tasks and situations.

The above effects are usually short-lived and cause no lasting harm and the individual quickly returns to normal. However, in some situations, pressures can be so intense that the effects of stress are more sustained and damaging and can lead to longer-term psychological problems and physical ill-health, such as:

- heart disease
- high blood pressure
- thyroid disorders
- ulcers
- depression
- post-traumatic stress disorder.

The workplace consequences of stress can lead to organisational problems. These include:

- industrial relations problems
- poor productivity and/or work performance
- poor timekeeping
- poor staff and client relationships
- increased absenteeism
- increased accident rates
- increased staff turnover.

How Significant is Stress at Work?

The Health and Safety Executive estimates that 10% of the workforce suffers from stress at any one time, resulting in British industry losing 90 million working days per annum, at a cost of £6 billion.

In July 1995, Labour Research reported that staff turnover and sickness absence related to stress costs employers £1.3 billion per annum and causes a loss of over 90 million working days per annum.

At an Industrial Society conference in September 1995, it was reported that stress-related problems could absorb the equivalent of between 5% and 10% of company profits.

In September 1995 the Chief Medical Officer, in his annual review of public health, stated that stress, after back pain, is now the most common cause of absence lasting more than 21 days.

The London Hazards Centre estimates that the cost to British Industry due to the increased incidence of work-related stress illnesses is £7 billion per annum.

An NOP survey in 1995 reported its finding that half of the country's workforce are under stress in their jobs.

An MSF union survey in 1995 of 412 workplaces in a variety of organisations found that:

- 60% of employees say they suffer from stress at work "very often" or "fairly often"
- twice as many women as men say that they suffer from stress at work very often
- 71% say that stress levels in their workplace are higher than five years ago, and 69% say they are higher than one year ago
- 86% of employees identified insufficient time to do the job as an important cause of stress.

According to a survey on stress at work by the Institute of Personnel & Development, nearly a third of workers would be willing to accept less pay for more leisure time.

A survey in 1994 by the Harris Research Institute revealed that British workers suffer more stress-related illnesses than any other European country; 60% of British workers complained of stress compared to 54% of their European counterparts.

Separate research reveals that a fifth of British workers have taken time off through work worries and the Leeds Occupational Health Forum referred to "a major epidemic sweeping through the region's workplaces in 1995, with as many as one in three employees suffering from stress-related problems and diseases".

The results of two surveys on stress were published early in 1996. These were by the Communication Managers' Association (CMA) and The Industrial Society (IS). Both reported rapid increases in stress.

The CMA represents employees from first line supervisor level to lower senior managers. The survey was of 1400 respondents and gives a snapshot of Post Office managers' views. Workplace issues reported to be "extremely stressful" or "stressful" included conflicting demands on time (89%), constant interruptions (87%), and securing the correct information (79%). Of the 1400 respondents, 59% reported disturbed sleep patterns, 55% headaches and 53% undue exhaustion. Some 60% of CMA members reported that they experienced an increase of up to 30% in stress levels.

The IS survey involved 699 personnel and HR managers. Two-thirds of respondents, and three-quarters in the financial sector, claim their organisation regards stress as part of the job. In addition, the survey revealed that 42% of companies regard problems outside work as the cause of their employees' stress but only 25% blame poor management. Increased absenteeism is believed to be the most damaging effect of stress by 75% of the managers, but only 7% measure the amount of absence caused by stress.

The Institute of Management Survey, in 1996, found that an estimated 270,000 people take time off each day because of work-related stress. This costs £7 billion a year taking into account all the consequences. Nine out of ten managers believe that job-related stress is adversely affecting morale, health and efficiency at work as well as their personal relationships. The most common causes of work-related stress were reported to be unreasonable deadlines (56%), office politics (51%), firing other members of staff (28%) and stress due to bullying behaviour/intimidation from colleagues was reported by 31% of female managers and 22% of male managers.

In the September 1996 Consumer Focus Survey it was found that stress in the workplace accounts for more than 40 million working days absence annually, at a cost to industry of £79 billion. Absenteeism due to stress is rising in 83% of firms. Middle management experience the highest levels of stress. Main causes of stress were increased responsibility or job merge (75%) and job insecurity (73%). Poor management skills were reported by 76% of respondents.

According to a survey of trade union Health and Safety representatives conducted in October 1996, two thirds of them reported that stress was the *main* health and safety issue at their workplace.

The findings of a 1997 Report and survey of occupational health workers commissioned by Zovirax included:

- an increase in workplace stress over the past 5 years reported in 89% of businesses
- a rise in stress-related absenteeism by 83% of the health workers questioned and $\frac{2}{3}$ of the firms seeing a lowering of employees' resistance to illness.

Dr Lewis, the stress consultant in the report, says that stress results in up to 85% of industrial accidents and 60% of crashes involving company cars. His tips to help employees keep stress under control are to:

- not try to be perfect and set oneself impossible targets
- escape to a private paradise in the imagination when the real world gets too stressful
- talk over problems with family and friends and laugh as much as possible
- note warning signs and minor ailments
- breath slowly and deeply at the first signs of stress
- know your "red buttons" — people and events that always make you stressed and should be prepared for in advance.

What Causes Stress?

There is no single cause of stress. Generally, harmful levels of stress are most likely to occur:

- where pressures pile on top of each other, or are prolonged
- where people feel trapped or unable to exert any control over the demands placed on them
- where people are confused by conflicting demands made on them

- where recessionary economic conditions cause job losses.

In the workplace, stress is likely to occur:
- where there is a high degree of uncertainty about employees' work, their objectives or their job and career prospects
- where work schedules are inflexible and over-demanding
- where there is prolonged conflict between individuals including sexual and racial harassment, bullying or where the staff are treated with contempt or indifference
- where there is a lack of understanding and leadership from managers and supervisors.

Insurance Brokers Sedgwick identified the following causes of stress in their research carried out in 1995:
- job insecurity
- lack of control over work
- too heavy or too light work schedules
- uncertainty over role
- lack of recognition
- poor communication
- playing no part in the decision-making
- poor relations with colleagues
- poor job specifications.

Specific Jobs

Jobs which are more emotionally demanding are inherently more stressful, for example:
- the emergency services
- employees exposed to violence and danger
- the social services.

Employees engaged in these jobs need special training and support. Having been exposed to stressful or other traumatic events, they may suffer post-traumatic stress disorder and require professional help to recover.

The Working Environment

Unpleasant physical conditions can lead to stress in employees, for example where there is:
- excessive noise, heat, humidity, vibration
- toxic or dangerous material or other workplace hazards which are not adequately controlled.

The Employer's Legal Duties

There is no specific legislation on controlling stress at work. However, employers are under both a statutory and common law duty to ensure the health and safety of their staff.

Under the **Health and Safety at Work, etc Act 1974** (HSWA) employers are under a duty to ensure, so far as is reasonably practicable, that their workplaces are safe and healthy. Note that criminal prosecution can result from breach of this obligation.

In *HSE v Firth Furnishings Ltd* (1995) (unreported), an employee's thumb was crushed in machinery and the accident was witnessed by another employee who was allowed to return to work on the same machine the next day. This employee subsequently became ill with post-traumatic stress syndrome. The company was found guilty of breaches of the HSWA in respect of both the original injury and the second employee's psychiatric condition caused by her anxiety in working on the same dangerous machine. The company was fined £2500 for each offence and ordered to pay the employees £2000 and £300 compensation respectively.

By virtue of the **Management of Health and Safety at Work Regulations 1992**, employers must make a suitable and sufficient assessment of the nature and scale of risks to health in their workplace and instigate steps to control any risks which are revealed by this health and safety audit.

The Common Law Position

Employers have a common law duty of care to provide their employees with a reasonably safe system of work and to take necessary steps to protect their workforce from risks that are reasonably foreseeable.

An employer who either fails to take the steps that a reasonable employer would take or acts in a way which a reasonable employer would not, may be held by the courts to be negligent.

In order to succeed in a work-related personal injury claim based on negligence, the plaintiff must prove each of the following four interrelated factors:

   (i)   that the employer failed in its duty of care towards the employee
   (ii) that injury resulted from that breach
   (iii) that the conditions at work caused the injury
   (iv) that the injury in question was reasonably foreseeable by the employer.

As it is well established that employers owe their employees a duty of care, this does not present a large hurdle to a plaintiff. The exact nature and scope of any injury resulting from the employer's breach has been judicially defined in *Petch v Customs and Excise Commissioners* [1993] ICR 789 and *Walker* (below) to include both physical and psychiatric injury to an employee. The duty to provide a safe system of work covers the *organisation* of the work. This includes the character and volume of the work as well as the urgency imposed by deadlines.

Not every type of injury, however, will lead to a successful award of damages. The injury must be one which is the result of stress *in the workplace*. There are a range of stress-related disorders, some physical such as headaches and raised blood pressure and some behavioural such as irritability and anxiety. A claimant would need to prove that the ailment, such as a nervous breakdown, was due to stress in the workplace and not due to some extrinsic cause such as a genetic or dietary problem, or domestic factors such as a marriage breakup. Similarly, other work which the employee does can be relevant in assessing potential liability and compensation.

An employer can only be liable for risks to an employee's health which are *foreseeable*. This means that the employer in question must be aware, or should have been aware, of the possibility that this particular employee was likely to suffer from a stress-related injury in that particular job. Much will depend on the circumstances of the case but where an employee has a history of stress-related illness, or is exhibiting the warning signs for the first time, a reasonable employer would address the risk and take the necessary preventative action. This may take a variety of forms such as a change in workload or pattern, retraining or counselling. Whether an employer has taken reasonable preventative steps will be judged on the magnitude of the risk, the cost and practicality of prevention and the seriousness for the individual involved.

Case Law on Stress

Walker v Northumberland County Council [1995] IRLR 35
The High Court held that the Local Authority employer was liable for the second nervous breakdown suffered by one of its Area Social Services Officers. The court decided that it was foreseeable that Mr Walker would suffer the second nervous breakdown when subjecting him to the same workload which caused his first breakdown. He should have been given the additional help that he had been promised but which never materialised. Mr Walker originally sought £200,000 compensation but subsequently accepted an out-of-court settlement of £175,000 and both sides dropped their appeals to the Court of Appeal.

Johnstone v Bloomsbury Health Authority [1991] IRLR 118

The Court of Appeal decided that the Health Authority was in breach of its implied duty to safeguard its employee's health and safety by requiring Dr Johnstone to work an average 88 hours per week. The excessive hours caused him stress, sleep deprivation and depression and subsequently led to an out-of-court settlement of £5600 damages by his former employers.

Pickering v Sussex Police (1995) (unreported)

A policeman who retired prematurely because of chronic depression successfully gained a disablement pension in addition to his retirement pension because he had been disabled by the stress suffered in the course of his work as a jailer at Brighton Magistrates' Court. He endured a general state of tension, threats, confrontation and constant scuffles and was attacked on several occasions.

Whitbread plc t/a Thresher v Gulleyes (EAT 478/92)

The EAT held that Thresher had failed in their duty towards Ms Gulleyes by failing to give her the necessary support and resources to do her job. Not only did she have to work an average of 76 hours per week as branch manager, but two of her most experienced staff were transferred to other branches in her absence and without her being consulted. Under this strain Ms Gulleyes requested a transfer, which was refused, thereupon resigned and successfully claimed constructive dismissal. There had been a fundamental breach of the implied duty of support, in that her employer had effectively prevented her from carrying out her contractual duties.

Chamberlain Vinyl Products Ltd v Patel [1996] ICR 113

Mr Patel was employed as a night shift operator. He arrived at work under the influence of drink and was unsteady on his feet. When his line manager approached him about this he reacted aggressively, physically attacking him by grabbing his throat. Mr Patel was sent home and subsequently interviewed by the works manager. During this interview Mr Patel revealed that he was under the care of a psychiatrist.

Although Mr Patel could clearly have been dismissed for gross misconduct, his employers decided to embark on a medical investigation into Mr Patel's behaviour. Medical feedback on Mr Patel's condition proved difficult to come by but eventually Mr Patel's doctor confirmed that he was suffering from recurrent depression and was under treatment, although there was no proof that the depression was work-related. Following contact between the employer and the company doctor, Mr Patel was dismissed for gross misconduct.

The industrial tribunal and the EAT held the dismissal to be unfair because, having begun a medical enquiry the employer had failed to investigate the matter properly and resolve some important issues about Mr Patel. As Mr Patel was in clear breach of the company's disciplinary rules by being violent and also drunk at work, there was no need for the employer to investigate Mr Patel's medical condition which didn't appear to be work-related. Thus there are clearly dangers in an employer taking this dual approach and not fully following each through to a proper conclusion. Note that the industrial tribunal reduced the compensation award by 65% for contributory fault by Mr Patel, although the case was remitted by the EAT on this point for technical reasons.

Hobbs v British Railways Board (EAT 340/94)

The EAT held that the employer had done what was necessary to protect an employee, Mr Hobbs, who was suffering from severe stress because a work colleague had been charged with indecently assaulting Mr Hobbs' stepdaughter. Mr Hobbs resigned because he wanted his colleague suspended pending the trial and his own request for a transfer had been refused by the management. However, the employer had minimised the contact between the two employees and Mr Hobbs had received reassurance and welfare. The employer had therefore taken reasonable steps to support its employee so that he could continue to do his job, albeit under stressful circumstances.

Robertson and Rough v The Forth Road Bridge Joint Board [1995] IRLR 251

Mr Robertson and Mr Rough both suffered psychiatric injury from a work-related incident and claimed damages from their employer. They witnessed the death of one of their colleagues in a freak accident on the bridge and suffered considerable nervous shock as a result. The Court of Session refused to extend the general duty of care owed by an employer to cover psychiatric injury caused to employees seeing a colleague killed or injured while at work.

Hegarty v EE Caladonia (1995) (unreported)

In December 1995, Mr William Hegarty lost his High Court claim that he had suffered psychiatric injuries during the Piper Alpha disaster. He witnessed the events unfold from a range of 100 metres and suffered post traumatic stress disorder (PTSD). But the court held that there was nothing that had happened aboard the support ship *Tharos* where he was which was likely to endanger his safety or welfare. Any fear which he had was not reasonable fear in the circumstances.

In January 1996, the Home Office awarded seven prisoners at Strangeways *ex gratia* payments of nearly £5000 each for PTSD which they claimed they suffered from witnessing the 1990 prison riot.

In June 1996, 14 police officers received a total of £1.2 million compensation for the psychological harm they suffered via PTSD arising out of the Hillsborough disaster. Five of the officers had been forced to leave the service due to their experiences.

Ballantyne v South Lanarkshire Council (1996) (unreported)

Ms Ballantyne, a deputy officer in charge of a retirement home, suffered depression and panic attacks caused by the behaviour of her manager. She was forced to take early retirement because of stress-related illness and was awarded £66,000 in damages.

Paxton v North Yorkshire Police (1996)

In September 1996, it was disclosed that an out-of-court settlement of £150,000 was paid to a superintendent who left the force suffering from stress which he alleged was work-related.

McKenzie v Royal Ordinance (1996)

A £125,000 out-of-court settlement of a PTSD claim was given to a shift supervisor who suffered PTSD due to regular exposure to fumes and blow outs at work. He was also responsible for evacuating the building in such circumstances.

How to Combat Stress

Employers need to adopt all reasonable measures to deal with stress in the workplace. The following guidelines should be followed.

1. A stress audit should be carried out to identify all potential workplace stresses.
2. Key personnel, such as managers and personnel staff should receive training to enable them to recognise stress-related problems in the workplace.
3. Employers should have a stress policy or guidelines to enable staff to know what to do if they are suffering from stress and how to get help. The policy might involve referrals to specialists and the elimination of particular stressors.

4. Employers should try to foster an atmosphere at work which encourages staff to ask for assistance when suffering from stress.

The Health and Safety Executive (HSE) *Guide for Employers* recommends:

*   ensuring that workplace stress is a problem which is understood and taken seriously

*   ensuring that staff know what job they have to do and are confident that they can do it properly; the job itself needs to be "do-able"

*   avoiding a management style which is inconsistent, exhibits indifference or bullying

*   avoiding long periods of high uncertainty

*   ensuring good two-way communication.

Much can be achieved by management being flexible, allowing scope for varying working conditions, treating staff fairly and ensuring that employees have the necessary skills, training and resources to do their job properly.

The HSE stresses the *business case* for employers reducing stress levels at work. Action on stress can be very cost-effective because it leads to:

−   better health

−   reduced sickness absence

−   increased performance and output

−   better relationships with colleagues and clients

−   lower staff turnover.

In December 1995, the Home Office announced that it was spending an estimated £20,000 on stress counsellors for its staff in British passport offices. The facility was available to all of the 1800 staff in the Passport Agency and was an attempt to improve morale, reduce staff turnover and increase productivity. Staff were to be fully supported to deal with negative and debilitating stress.

Summary

- It is estimated that British industry loses 90 million working days per annum from stress-related absence, at a cost of £6 billion.

- Stress is now believed to be the most common cause of absence lasting more than 21 days, after back pain.

- There are a number of recognised factors — both physical and psychological — which cause stress in the workplace and certain jobs are inherently more stressful.

- Employers are under a duty to ensure the health and safety of their staff, including protecting their employees from stressful working conditions where possible.

- An employer can only be liable for risks to an employee's health which are foreseeable.

- Employers should adopt all reasonable measures to deal with stress in the workplace.

- There is a good business case for employers reducing stress levels at work because it leads to better staff health, reduced sickness and absence, and increased performance and output.

Useful Reading

Stress at Work — A guide for Employers is available from:
HSE Books
PO Box 1999
Sudbury
Suffolk CO10 6FS
Tel: 01787 881165

Coping with Stress at Work Pack is available from:
Royal College of Psychiatrists
Tel: 0151-632 0662

7   Misconduct

Introduction

Misconduct at work can arise as a result of an employee's breach of his or her employer's rules regulating staff behaviour or as a result of an employee's refusal to obey a lawful and reasonable order.

Breach of Employer's Disciplinary Rules

An employer would be well-advised to devise a set of disciplinary rules to inform staff what is and what is not viewed as acceptable conduct.

Paragraph 6 of the ACAS Code of Practice on Disciplinary Procedure and Practice states:

> it is unlikely that any set of disciplinary rules can cover all circumstances that may arise: moreover the rules required will vary according to particular circumstances such as the type of work, working conditions and size of establishment. When drawing up rules the aim should be to specify clearly and concisely those necessary for the efficient and safe performance of work, and for the maintenance of satisfactory relations in the workforce and between employees and management. Rules should not be so general as to be meaningless.

According to the ACAS advisory handbook, *Discipline at Work*, the rules should cover such things as:

- timekeeping
- absence
- health and safety
- gross misconduct
- use of company facilities

- discrimination.

Such rules must be readily understandable and properly communicated to all staff. Section 1 of the **Employment Rights Act 1996** (ERA), dictates that employees should be given a written statement which includes any disciplinary rules which apply. An employer is free to devise a list containing examples of behaviour which constitute examples of gross misconduct and should specify that the list is not exhaustive.

According to the IRS survey the offences most commonly listed as gross misconduct, in order of incidence, are:

- assault
- theft
- fraud
- sexual harassment
- indecent conduct
- serious health and safety breaches
- alcohol/drugs misuse
- helping competitors/unauthorised disclosure of information
- tampering with time recording offences
- incidents leading to criminal convictions.

However, even where there are no express rules covering certain misbehaviour, it does not follow that dismissal will be unfair. In *CA Parsons & Co. Ltd v McLoughlin* [1978] IRLR 65, it was held to be fair to dismiss an employee for fighting even though the employer had no specific rule forbidding it. The EAT stated:

> *it ought not to be necessary for anybody to have in black and white in the form of a rule that a fight is something which is going to be regarded very gravely by management.*

Refusal to Obey a Reasonable Order

The employee's contract of employment is of vital importance in assessing what orders an employer can issue in terms of work demands. Apart from the express terms, custom and practice can be important as can any incorporated collective agreements or works rules.

Where an employee fails to carry out his or her usual duties, a dismissal is likely to be fair for breach of contract. In *Coendoz v Midland Bank Ltd* [1975] IRLR 172, the employee's refusal to do a job was motivated by annoyance at being overlooked for promotion.

If an employee refuses to switch to different work than usual but which is still within his or her contract of employment, this can also amount to breach of contract and lead to a subsequent dismissal. So, if the employee refuses to abide by the terms of a mobility clause in his or her contract, as in *Hann and Edwards v Crittall-Hope Ltd* [1972] IRLR 102, this can result in a fair dismissal. Note that a "work to rule" can be regarded as a form of industrial action and a breach of contract, since it is calculated to disrupt the smooth running of the employer's business (*Secretary of State for Employment v ASLEF* [1972] ICR 7).

An employee is only obliged to carry out orders which are both legitimate and lawful and need not put him or herself in danger or assist in the commission of a criminal offence.

Malingerers

A malingerer is somebody who pretends, produces or protracts illness in order to escape work. Since this is a form of deception, management are entitled to view it seriously and apply the normal disciplinary rules and procedures. Whether it constitutes gross misconduct depends on the circumstances of the case but, in any event, it is necessary to follow all the standard disciplinary procedures before dismissal. Therefore, there must be a comprehensive investigation and the employee must be given a chance to respond to the allegations, together with a subsequent right of appeal against any decision made.

In *Bailey v BP Kent Oil Refinery* [1980] IRLR 287, it was held to be fair to dismiss an employee who feigned illness by self-certifying he had a gastric stomach in order to take time off for a week's holiday in Majorca, which had previously been refused.

In *Hutchinson v Enfield Rolling Mills Ltd* [1981] IRLR 318, Hutchinson had produced a doctor's sick note but during the time he was off ill, he travelled to Brighton to participate in a union demonstration. His dismissal was held to be fair despite the doctor's sick note because the employer could demonstrate evidence to the contrary.

Should the absence be of a prolonged period, management may require the individual to attend a consultation with the company doctor, or a doctor nominated by the company, in order to get a second opinion.

Behaviour Outside Work

As a general rule, an employee's private life is their own concern. However, there are some forms of behaviour occurring away from work, such as violence, dishonesty and sexual impropriety, which may constitute misconduct and which can put an employee's job in jeopardy.

Such behaviour can have a significant adverse impact on the employer's business from a number of angles. The incident may attract damaging publicity to the organisation, it may call into question the suitability of the employee to remain in his or her particular job and it might result in friction with other employees.

An employer who decides to dismiss an employee for outside misconduct may use the "conduct" ground within s.98(2)(b) of the ERA or the "some other substantial reason" ground within s.98(1)(b) of the ERA as a defence to an unfair dismissal claim. The employer needs to be able to show that the behaviour in question actually took place and that this has seriously damaged the working relationship between the employer and the employee.

The ACAS Code of Practice on Discipline, Practice and Procedures urges caution where employees are either charged, remanded in custody or convicted of criminal offences. It states that employees should not *automatically* be dismissed from their jobs in such cases, although of course much depends on the circumstances. However, while it may be good policy for an employer to wait until an employee is convicted before deciding to dismiss, it is possible to dismiss immediately where the employer has gained a reasonable belief in guilt, having carried out a reasonable investigation into the facts. The employer's required standard of proof is only "on the balance of probabilities", as compared to the criminal standard of proof which is "beyond reasonable doubt". Note that because of these differing standards, a subsequent acquittal does not necessarily render a previous dismissal unfair.

When taking disciplinary action against an employee for outside misconduct, all the normal rules of natural justice must be applied to ensure that the individual is treated fairly and short cuts can render the subsequent dismissal unfair.

Sexual Misconduct

The whole range of sexual offences can result in an employee being viewed as *unsuitable* to remain in his or her job. For instance, a teacher's conviction for indecent assault or indecent exposure. Apart from this, there is the reaction of colleagues who may be hostile or refuse to work with the individual. These are all legitimate concerns for an employer.

Violence

Off-duty fighting and other violent behaviour can justify workplace disciplinary proceedings because it can tarnish the reputation of the business and can cause alarm to other employees who may feel threatened by the presence of an aggressive or unpredictable colleague. The employer's response to violent behaviour will depend on many factors, such as where the incident took place and who was involved. It would clearly be an aggravating factor if the violence was against another employee, such as the employee's team leader, despite it being off the premises and outside working hours. Similarly, a propensity to violence would be incompatible with certain job posts, such as a police officer or security guard.

Dishonesty

Offences such as theft, fraud, deception and corruption arising out of one's private life can clearly have a knock-on effect at work depending on the circumstances. The relevant factors are:
- the particular nature of the business, eg a bank
- the risk to the employer's business because of the employee's job, eg a payroll clerk
- the likelihood of damage to the employer's reputation in the eyes of the public or its clients.

Political Activities

Affiliations and activities connected to certain parties, even though not in themselves illegal, can prove to be incompatible with the holding of certain jobs, especially where there are race considerations.

In *London Borough of Greenwich v Dell* (EAT 7/95), the EAT upheld an industrial tribunal's finding of fact that the dismissal of one of the Borough's caretakers because of his political affiliations to the British National Party was unfair. However, the EAT refused to order his re-engagement.

Group Dismissals

Occasionally, employers are faced with a situation where there has been behaviour in the workplace which justifies dismissal for misconduct but the employer is unable to pinpoint the individual responsible. Where the culprit is one of a group of potential suspects, an employer may be tempted to make a blanket dismissal of all those in the group and to recruit replacements rather than spend time trying to establish exactly who was the wrongdoer. This understandable approach should only be a last resort, however, and an employer who adopts this strategy too hastily could expect to receive multiple claims for unfair dismissal as a consequence.

The most common situations where the question of group dismissal arises are cases of theft from the employer and vandalism at work. In both of these circumstances there may not be decisive evidence to put the blame on any one individual but a small group of employees might all be legitimately under suspicion by the employer. In such situations it is vital for the employer to satisfy the five conditions governing fair group dismissals established by the Employment Appeal Tribunal in *Parr v Whitbread plc* [1990] IRLR 39. These are that:

- there must have been an act committed which, if committed by an individual, would justify dismissal
- the employer must have made a reasonable and sufficiently thorough investigation into the matter and adopted appropriate procedures
- as a consequence of the investigation, the employer must reasonably believe that more than one person could have committed the act in question

- the employer must have acted reasonably in identifying the group of employees who could have committed the act and each member of the group must have been individually capable of doing so, and

- the employer could not reasonably identify the individual offender from within the group.

Although the size and administrative resources of an employer are always relevant in judging whether a dismissal is fair, all employers should investigate the facts very carefully in blanket dismissal cases because such dismissals necessarily involve innocent persons as well as the guilty one. In the case of a large organisation it would be reasonable to expect the employer to have carried out in-depth internal surveillance before resorting to blanket dismissals but even small employers must first have carried out some investigation before dismissing a group of employees.

In *Walker v Lakhdari t/a Mayfair Newsagency* (EAT 2/91) (unreported), it was held that it was fair for a small employer who had suffered cash deficiencies of £5000 and faced financial problems as a result to warn all the staff that, if the losses continued for another month, he would be forced to dismiss them all and subsequently did so. He had made unavailing checks to discover which one or more of them were stealing from him.

The fact that some staff are not dismissed from among the group of potentially guilty ones does not automatically make the dismissal of the remainder unfair providing the employer can show solid and sensible grounds for differentiating between the employees. In *Frames Snooker Centre v Boyce* [1992] IRLR 472, the employer dismissed two out of his three managers following the third burglary at the centre, which the police thought was an inside job. The third manager was the proprietor's daughter and he had complete confidence in her honesty. The dismissal of the two managers were held to be fair and the EAT said that there is no "all or none" principle which an employer must follow.

A similar decision was reached in *Evans v Dista Products Ltd* (EAT 1227/94), where the employer was held to have fairly dismissed three employees from within a group of at least eight who were caught drinking and gambling on the company premises. When they were discovered they hastily dispersed thereby making it impossible for the employer to identify all the employees who were involved. The employer's investigation disclosed sufficient evidence, however, to implicate the three who were dismissed even if others who were undoubtedly equally guilty were getting away scot-free because of the lack of evidence as to their identity.

Moonlighting

An employer is entitled to expect loyal and faithful service from its employees. This responsibility can be called into question where a member of staff is discovered to be moonlighting in his or her spare-time, in particular where the work is being performed for a competing business.

Implied into every employee's contract of employment is a duty of good faith and fidelity and an employee can be in breach of this term by undertaking outside work in his or her own time. An employment contract relies on a relationship of trust between the parties and an employee should concentrate his or her efforts in the best interest of the employer. It is common for contracts to contain express terms regulating the performance of outside work by employees but the law recognises that, in principle, an employee should be allowed to earn additional income outside his or her main job. As a result, prohibitions can be viewed as being in unlawful restraint of trade and thus void. An employer would have to demonstrate that it had some legitimate business interest to protect and the employee's outside work unreasonably compromised this. Some contracts require staff to seek permission from their employer before they undertake any other paid work and such permission should not be unreasonably withheld. Key issues would be whether the proposed work interfered with the employer's business and to what extent this was so.

Even where there is an express term prohibiting employees from doing outside work, a dismissal for contravening the rule might not be a fair one where the employer was aware of the moonlighting and did nothing to prevent it or otherwise gave tacit approval. Similarly, not all outside work, even for a rival, is necessarily in competition to that of the employer, so a proper investigation and evaluation of the facts is required before taking hasty action. There should be a definite conflict of interest involved or the risk of significant harm to the employer's own business.

Where a full-time employee is also working elsewhere, other considerations can arise. The outside work might seriously affect the employee's ability to perform his or her main job satisfactorily and the accumulation of long working hours can have health and safety implications both for the employee and for his or her colleagues. This would be especially true where machinery is to be operated and where the employee arrives at work already tired as a result of the other work. This situation is one which a team leader should be attuned to and should investigate as a matter of priority if, and when, a pattern begins to emerge. Increased absenteeism can also be an indicator of outside work, as can the prevalence of injuries resulting in time off being taken for sickness. A gradual fall-off in performance or attendance requires an interview by the team leader to investigate the cause. Frequently, information about an employee moonlighting is received from other sources and this needs to be followed up to establish the likelihood of its truth, the employer only needing ultimately to be satisfied on the balance of probabilities.

It is worth remembering that employees who are particularly low-paid might be compelled to supplement their main job to make ends meet and an employer should recognise this. This does not mean, however, that an employer should tolerate poor time-keeping or employees leaving early in order to fit in their other work commitments, unless this has been agreed in advance. Where there is no prior agreement, such behaviour should be treated as a disciplinary issue.

It is sensible for an employer to devise and implement a policy dealing specifically with moonlighting and to draw this fully to the attention of all the staff. Team leaders will have a crucial role in monitoring compliance with the policy and ultimately enforcing it through stated procedures, which should include an informal first stage. In many cases a warning following discovery of the facts by the employer is sufficient to prevent the employee from moonlighting in the future.

Employees' Loyalty

One of the most important implied contractual duties placed on an employee is that of loyalty towards his or her employer. When an employee is taken on, he or she has a duty to serve faithfully and not to act in any way which is detrimental to his or her employer's commercial interests. The employment relationship is based on trust between the parties and an employee who breaches this trust may be dismissed for gross misconduct and breach of contract as a result.

The relationship of trust and loyalty endures throughout the contract of employment and can be compromised by an employee in a variety of ways. Employees must act both honestly and in good faith in relation to their employer. Their primary duty is towards their employer's business and not their own interests. Accordingly, they must not make a secret profit from their work and they are accountable for any money received by them in connection with their employer's business. This is particularly relevant where staff have responsibility for awarding contracts and commissioning work, and who may be offered bribes, sweeteners or backhanders by outsiders seeking to influence them. Similarly, any outside connection the employee has with a supplier or customer, or potential one, whether the link is family or commercially based, should be disclosed to his or her employer in advance of any contracts being awarded.

An employee who receives commercial information in the course of his or her job holds this on trust for the employer. Equally, where an employee makes a discovery or invention in the course of his or her job, this is the property of the employer, who may also own the copyright in work produced by the employee, who is not then free to exploit and market it on a personal basis.

As regards confidential information which an employee possesses, or has access to in the course of his or her job, an employee is under an implied duty not to disclose this to third parties, whether for gain or otherwise. This duty can continue after the employee has left the job where it relates to trade secrets and other commercially sensitive matter.

One of the most blatant examples of disloyalty arises when an employee undertakes work for a business rival of his or her employer, or sets up in competition to his or her employer in his or her spare time. Such behaviour would justify dismissal from a number of angles. Moonlighting in itself is not necessarily damaging to an employer's business interests, but any activity by an employee which diverts business away from the employer, or is in competition to it, is in breach of the employee's implied duty of loyalty. A good illustration is the case of *Adamson v B & L Cleaning Services Ltd* [1995] IRLR 193, in which the foreman of a cleaning firm was held to have broken his implied contractual duty by tendering personally for a contract currently held by his employer at a time when the contract was up for renewal.

Undermining the employer from within the organisation can also arise where an employee is plotting to leave his or her job and is making distinct plans to do so at the employer's expense. Much depends on the nature and extent of the employee's schemes but in *Marshall v Industrial Systems & Control Ltd* [1992] IRLR 294, it was held to be gross misconduct for a managing director to plan his own future venture and try to persuade another senior manager to join him in an attempt to deprive the company of their best client.

On the other hand, it was not considered disloyal in *Laughton & Hawley v Bapp Industrial Supplies Ltd* [1986] IRLR 245, for two employees merely to plan to set up together in competition with their employer once they had both left their jobs. There had been no abuse of confidential knowledge, no misuse of their employer's time and they were not subject to any other contractual constraints.

Workplace Affairs

When two members of staff have an affair, or a relationship which goes beyond being platonic, this can present the employer with a particularly sensitive problem. In fact, many employees marry their work colleagues and this reflects the social dimension of a typical working environment. Others form an attachment through working in close proximity together for long periods of the day, week by week. In principle, there is nothing wrong with this and indeed an employer should avoid meddling in the personal life of its staff. However, relationships between staff can present particular difficulties for management which they will need to address sooner or later.

One obvious problem which can arise is that the two individuals may become distracted from their work in each other's presence, with consequent loss in efficiency. Their behaviour may be distracting to others or become the subject of time-consuming gossip at work. An employer clearly has the right to regulate staff behaviour on the premises, especially where individuals are not fulfilling their roles properly or are guilty of misconduct. In some situations, health and safety standards could be compromised, particularly where concentration is required when operating machinery.

If two members of staff are having an affair and they are at different levels of seniority within the organisation, the higher grade employee may show favouritism towards the lower grade employee in their working relationship. Even if it is not true, he or she may face accusations of favouritism from others, the suspicions of which it may be difficult to disprove. This would be especially true where internal staff promotions are concerned. An employer has to ensure that decision-making affecting competing staff is based on fair and open competition. Team leaders have to be aware of the possibility of relationships between staff which could compromise fairness and must declare an interest where they themselves are directly involved.

Some employers try to control workplace affairs by including a rule discouraging or expressly forbidding them in the contracts of employment of their staff. If an affair is discovered, this can then be dealt with as an act of misconduct arising from disobedience, with resulting disciplinary sanctions such as disciplinary transfer or dismissal. However, even where contractual rules exist, taking disciplinary action on the basis of an alleged affair is fraught with difficulties. A dismissed employee may well bring a claim for unfair dismissal or constructive dismissal on the basis that there is no real proof that an intimate relationship actually exists, let alone one that has a potentially detrimental effect at work.

An employer taking disciplinary action in respect of a workplace affair may also face accusations of sex discrimination where both parties involved are not treated the same. A situation which could easily arise where the female employee was in the more junior post at work and is the one transferred away to a different department in order to split up the couple.

Another potential difficulty could arise where an employee has an affair with someone from a rival organisation. Here the danger for the employer is that of the potential for leakage of confidential information between the two employees. In such cases, it can be fair to dismiss the individuals involved but only as a last resort and only after the proper procedures have been followed.

Whatever the situation, team leaders should not jump to conclusions about their staff and only initiate disciplinary action where a relationship has an adverse impact on the efficient running of the business.

Office Parties

It is important to think carefully about the likely behaviour of staff at office parties. Although it is inevitable that most employees will "let their hair down" on such occasions, managers need to maintain overall standards of staff behaviour lest things go too far, with possible legal consequences.

The first task of the team leader is to ensure that the staff for whom he or she is responsible are fully aware of the in-house rules that exist about employee conduct, whether on site or away from work. If an office function is to be held at a local club, hotel or restaurant, then the public image of the organisation could be on the line. The business reputation of the company could also suffer because of the antics of the staff, so a clear reminder to staff of their responsibilities when attending company functions of any type off the premises is a prudent step.

Staff who are in a supervisory position have a special duty to set a good example and their ability to manage their own staff could be jeopardised by their questionable conduct at an office party. In *Focus DIY Ltd v Nicholson* [1994] IDS Brief 543, it was held to be fair to dismiss a deputy manager for smoking cannabis in front of other company employees at an office party held at a local hotel. Any reasonable employer could have come to the conclusion that this member of staff's authority to manage had been damaged beyond repair.

The role of the employer leading up to an incident of staff misconduct should not be ignored. If there is a bar paid for by the employer, then drunken behaviour by staff is more than a distinct possibility. This was a key factor in the decision in *Whitbread Beer Company Ltd v Williams* [1996] IRLB 560, in which it was held to be unfair to dismiss three employees for their admittedly deplorable conduct at one of their employer's hotels.

Equally, the attitude of the employer to previous acts of employee misbehaviour, albeit in a social context such as the office Christmas party, is important. In *Dixons Stores Group Ltd v Dwan and O'Byrne* [1994] IRLB 511, two area managers were held to have been unfairly dismissed for performing a "particularly lewd act" at the office Christmas party. This was because there had been a history of similar behaviour in which "turns" by employees had taken place, some of which had resulted in complaints of sexual harassment. Furthermore, during the incident in question, the two employees were encouraged by a divisional director. Although there had been a change in the company's management thinking about the behaviour of staff at company functions, this change in attitude had not been communicated to the staff. It is vital that management spell out to all staff the type of behaviour that will not be tolerated and which could result in their dismissal. Where it appears that some misconduct has arisen, a proper investigation into the incident is required, followed by a fair disciplinary procedure.

It should also be remembered that an employer can become directly responsible for the actions of its staff in several ways. If staff cause damage to outside property during an office party, then the organising employer may be liable to pay for the resulting cost of the vandalism. Similarly, an employer may be found to be vicariously liable for acts of harassment, particularly sexual harassment, which can easily arise at an office party. This can result in unlimited compensation being awarded to staff who are the victims of such behaviour and employees need to be aware of the dangers of their conduct at staff social events crossing the line of what is acceptable.

Vandalism

Many employers have express rules stating that if an employee wilfully damages or misuses company property, this shall constitute gross misconduct. An employee who is bored or who has a grievance against his or her employer often has ample opportunity to cause considerable damage to valuable property such as computer equipment.

Acts of industrial sabotage can include flooding the premises by turning on taps, or starting fires. Such antics are not only gross misconduct but can also amount to a criminal offence. Often, though, an employee's behaviour is not intended to cause significant harm or disruption to his or her employer and is viewed by the culprit as "high jinks" or "skylarking". Even so, behaviour which starts as a practical joke can have serious repercussions. Interfering with fire or security alarm systems can appear to be just a "lark" but should be viewed seriously by managers. If damage to equipment is purely accidental and is careless rather than malicious, a warning may be more appropriate than dismissal.

In all cases of vandalism, a thorough investigation is required in an attempt to identify those responsible. An employer only needs to form a reasonable belief in an employee's guilt in order to take disciplinary action against him or her.

Stubborn and Unco-operative Employees

Employees have an implied duty to carry out their work with reasonable care and skill. Where an employee is behaving at work in an unco-operative or negative way and this is having a detrimental effect on the efficiency of the organisation, an employer may view this as a disciplinary matter. An employee's non-co-operation could be viewed as a challenge to managerial authority or it may simply be a case of his or her particular attitude to work.

Stubbornness can arise through a failure to obey instructions or carrying them out "to the letter" in an obstructive manner.

An employee's lack of co-operation may be the result of a stubborn unwillingness to update his or her skills. An employer can reasonably expect its staff to move with the times and adapt to new working practices and techniques. Alternatively, it may be due to a lack of motivation, in which case the employer needs to decide how best to remedy this. This could be by method of reward which will enhance the employees' self-worth. If this fails, it may be necessary to use the disciplinary system in order to improve performance.

Employers faced with stubbornness from an employee should investigate the position, discuss it fully with the employee, set performance targets and a timescale for improvement, monitor performance and meet again to review.

Personality Clashes

Where close co-operation between employees is required and individuals clash on a regular basis, it may be sensible to separate them, where this is operationally feasible and doesn't lead to contractual difficulties, in the interests of efficiency and harmony.

An employer needs to investigate personality clashes in an attempt to find out the underlying reasons. By definition, two or more employees have to be involved for there to be a personality clash and an employer must behave in a fair and consistent manner towards each one. Having investigated, it may be necessary to warn all those concerned about their future behaviour but if one employee is found to be more to blame than the rest, it could be fair to dismiss that individual and warn the others.

Gambling

Many employers expressly prohibit any form of gambling by staff on the company premises. Although employees have the right to work breaks at various intervals, and should be encouraged to relax, gambling can lead to tensions which can breed hostility within a work setting. Typically, card playing is the most likely form of gambling since games are easy to arrange and with no physical disruption to the workplace. In *Evans v Dista Products Ltd* (EAT 1227/94), the EAT held that it was fair to dismiss three employees caught playing cards and drinking in a locked room on company premises, contrary to express company rules.

One problem associated with gambling is that it can lead to intimidation, debt, frustration and anger between employees. It also encourages the staff to bring sums of money to work which they would otherwise not do. This increases the likelihood of theft and informal money lending.

Employers should be vigilant if gambling at work is prohibited and should make sure that employees are fully aware of their stance on it. It would be appropriate to issue formal warnings to staff involved in breach of the rules, although dismissal could result if the behaviour is repeated or accompanied by other behaviour such as violence, deception or other dishonesty.

Lateness

Where an employee is late for work on an isolated occasion, an employer should formally enquire as to the reason, which may be due to circumstances beyond the employee's control, in which case an employer might decide to take no action in the circumstances.

However, where an employee is repeatedly late for work, an employer needs to try to ascertain the underlying cause for this and to listen to any explanations advanced. Help or assistance might be needed where the employee has a personal or domestic problem.

Nevertheless, an employer cannot allow such a situation to continue indefinitely without improvement. A warning can be issued about future timekeeping and this should state that the employee's job will be in jeopardy if there is no improvement. A review period should be set and the employee's timekeeping record monitored.

Lateness can cause irritation and resentment among other employees and must be dealt with by management. Any steps taken to combat lateness must be applied consistently to all employees, otherwise allegations of favouritism will surface.

Insolence

Abusive and insolent behaviour is a form of misconduct and can ultimately damage the working relationship between the employee and the employer. In rare cases, a single instance of insolence can justify dismissal. Much will depend on the context of the incident and the background to it.

In *Tresham v Newport Components Ltd* [1988] IRLB 349, an employee with a previously good work record who used obscene language to her supervisor who had criticised her, was held to have been unfairly dismissed. Not only was this an isolated incident but there was no challenge to the authority of management.

Under certain circumstances, insolence can be viewed as gross misconduct, such as where it takes place in public and is witnessed by others, or where it could cause commercial harm to the business.

For example, in *Barker v Collina Products Ltd* [1988] IRLB 349, it was held to be fair to dismiss a bricklayer who used foul language to the wife of a client who was a Church of England clergyman.

When faced with insolence from an employee, the first stage should be to investigate the cause to ascertain if the behaviour in question is completely out of character. If so, the insolence may be an indication of stress, domestic problems, misuse of drink or drugs, or provocation by another employee. An employer should carefully listen to both sides of any story before coming to a decision on how to proceed. When challenged about his or her behaviour, an employee may voluntarily apologise but if he or she doesn't, management should warn the employee about his or her future conduct.

Theft and Fraud

Theft may be from the employer or from an employee's colleagues, or arise outside the workplace. However it arises, it is an indication of an employee's dishonesty and this can affect the trust in which the employee is held. Fraud can arise where individuals seek to deceive their employers, for instance by the fabrication of expenses or overtime claims or by "clocking" of timecards. Where an employee handles money on behalf of others, for instance a cashier or bookkeeper, there is scope for dishonest misappropriation.

Such behaviour constitutes gross misconduct and providing an employer undertakes a proper disciplinary procedure, it is probable that dismissal of the employee in question will be within the range of reasonable responses open to the employer.

Power to Search Staff

Employers have no inherent right to search their staff and should be particularly wary of attempting to search staff against their will. An employer who tries to reserve the right to search in the contract of employment must still proceed very carefully and should be fully aware of the pitfalls involved.

An employer may have the inclination to search an employee, or his or her possessions or vehicle because the employee is suspected of theft from the employer or from another employee. It is imperative to remember that an employer only has the same powers in this respect as any other member of the public and may not forcibly detain a member of staff on suspicion in order to question or search him or her.

Where an employer wants to reserve the right to search an employee, this should be expressly stated in the contract and it should be spelt out in what circumstances the power can be exercised and by whom. The scope of the power of search should be outlined and may extend, for instance, to the employee's locker or his or her car in the firm's car park. The employee should be made to sign the contract at the start of the job, thus indicating acceptance of the terms contained within it.

Where there is no express clause dealing with the power to search, it may be implied through the custom and practice of the particular employer. It is also often the case in an industry where employees handle high value, portable items, such as jewellery. However, it is better to include a contractual power and to bring this to the attention of all the staff.

Employers must be careful when they exercise the power of search. They should avoid allegations of victimisation, particularly where they have the power to search at random. In other situations they should only search where it is strictly necessary and where they are in a position to justify their actions. The search itself should be conducted in a controlled way and take place away from other employees. The person conducting the search of an employee should be of the same sex and it is advisable to have a witness present.

Even where there is a contractual power of search, permission to do so should be sought first. If the employee refuses to give permission, he or she should be warned that this is a breach of contract and that disciplinary action will be taken because of his or her refusal. Allowing a search to be conducted may be the only way that the employee can dispel the employer's suspicions and this should be made clear to the individual concerned, so that it is very much in his or her interest to co-operate fully.

In the event of a refusal, the employer, and all those participating in the search, should be mindful of the potential dangers in proceeding. An employee might bring a claim of:

- assault and battery
- indecent assault
- false imprisonment
- harassment or victimisation.

Team leaders are often directly involved in cases where it may be desirable to search staff. They should ensure that the necessary power of search exists before doing so and may legitimately refuse to carry out an order to search a colleague where the order is unreasonable or unauthorised.

Violence at Work

Employers owe a duty of care towards their staff to ensure that they are reasonably safe at work. Violence in the workplace is on the increase and employers must take steps to deal with the very real possibility that a violent incident involving one of their staff may occur without warning, with important legal consequences for all concerned.

Staff can be at risk of being involved in a violent incident with a member of the public, a customer or client or with a work colleague. "Violence" has been variously defined as "any incident in which an employee is abused, threatened or assaulted" as a result of which there is a direct challenge to his or her safety, health or well-being. Exposure to violent and aggressive behaviour at work, or the threat of it, is clearly an important health and safety issue and the **Management of Health and Safety at Work Regulations 1992** require an employer to conduct a risk assessment and adopt procedures in order to reduce the likelihood of such risks to staff.

By virtue of both the common law and the **Health and Safety at Work, etc Act 1974** (HSWA), employers must take such steps so as to ensure that their staff are reasonably safe from dangers that are reasonably foreseeable. The employer's exact duty in this respect will be determined by a variety of factors, such as the nature of the employee's job and the potential risk of violence associated with doing that work. The size of the employer's undertaking is also relevant but small employers still owe a duty of care to their staff.

Violence from Outsiders

According to the Suzy Lamplugh Trust, violent crime in the workplace accounts for 25% of all violent crime and three-quarters of violent incidents are assaults on staff by members of the public. Staff working in certain occupations face a greater degree of risk of violence from contact with the public and this amounts to a foreseeable danger which such employers are obliged to minimise. Research by the British Retail Consortium reveals the scale of potential risk of violent attack on staff who work in shops. There were over 300,000 incidents of threats of violence or abuse, levelled at staff in one year and 11,000 staff were actually involved in violent incidents at work, nearly 60% of which were the result of attempts to prevent shoplifting. The incidence of violent robbery and till snatches is rising and more than 1500 staff were injured during the course of 16,000 such incidents.

Health Service personnel are also at risk of violence at work and a survey by Unison in 1996 found that 40% of NHS staff had experienced violence at work in the previous year. Staff working in Benefit Offices also face clearly foreseeable risks of violence from the public which they serve. In all these types of workplace environments, it is incumbent on employers to take suitable measures to ensure the welfare of their staff and this includes providing training for staff in how to deal with the range of potentially violent situations which can arise. The Thresher off-licence chain, in keeping with others in their industry, provide comprehensive training for their staff to help them deal with threatened and actual violence by customers.

The provision of protective screens or equipment to shield staff from potential aggressors is considered essential in many working environments and it is also important to appreciate that staff can be placed under considerable stress when working in potentially hazardous conditions where the threat or *perceived* threat of violence towards staff is real.

Staff who are faced with such working conditions may ultimately resign and complain of constructive dismissal against their employer, with the potential for compensation. For instance, in *Keys v Shoefayre Ltd* [1978] IRLR 476, an employee who resigned because of the failure by management to take sensible precautions to ensure staff safety in the wake of two robberies on the premises, which was situated in a crime-ridden locality, succeeded because their inaction was held to be a fundamental breach of contract towards him. In such situations, the employer then has the additional cost of recruiting a replacement.

Violence from Colleagues

The risk of facing violence at work may come about from contact with other staff. Behaving in an aggressive, threatening or violent manner at work can clearly constitute an act of gross misconduct but this should still be spelt out expressly to all staff in their contracts of employment, or referred to as an example of gross misconduct in the company's staff handbook. The employer's disciplinary procedures should be followed to investigate incidents of violence between staff and to ensure that those involved receive a proper hearing and a chance to explain their conduct. In many cases, it will transpire that there was provocation involved or equal blame between several employees and this, together with the respective disciplinary records of those involved, will frequently determine the disciplinary penalties imposed. However, it was confirmed by the EAT in *Ullah v United Glass* (EAT 317/92) that an employer is entitled to take a firm line on violence between staff where this is considered by the employer to be blatant misconduct, and this could arise where it was a first offence or where there was nothing to show which of two employees was the most blameworthy.

An employer is entitled to view violence by staff as compromising health and safety in the workplace and this is especially relevant where an incident takes place near machinery or involves or distracts those in control of machinery. Under HSWA, employees are under a duty not to do anything to endanger themselves or their colleagues by their behaviour in the workplace.

Employers might be viewed as negligent if they appoint an individual with a known propensity for violent and aggressive behaviour. This can include a previous history of off-duty as well as work-related violent conduct. Pre-employment checks can go some way towards revealing an individual's violent profile through the disclosure of unspent criminal convictions for violent offences. The presence of such an individual at work may also have an unsettling effect on staff, who might fear that they are liable to be threatened or attacked. Such a member of staff could not be regarded as a "competent" appointment in the context of health and safety legislation.

An employer should make it clear to all staff that intimidatory, threatening or harassing behaviour by one employee towards another is considered unacceptable and may constitute a breach of the company's harassment or bullying code. Such misconduct will render the culprit liable to summary dismissal.

Special training is required to ensure that those staff who have a supervisory or security function at work behave in a responsible fashion when exercising that role. An employer can be vicariously liable for the behaviour of its staff when they are acting in the course of their employment. So the company could also be sued for compensation if an over-zealous security officer were to assault a fellow employee who was suspected of stealing from the premises.

Summary

- An employee's contract of employment is vital in assessing what orders an employer can issue.

- An employee is only obliged to carry out legitimate and lawful orders and need not put him or herself in danger or assist with a crime.

- Rules must be easy to understand and be properly communicated to all staff.

- Some forms of behaviour, such as violence, dishonesty and sexual impropriety, may put an employee's job in jeopardy even if they take place outside work.

- Employers should regard "group dismissals" as a last resort, given that they may result in multiple claims for unfair dismissal.

- An employee's responsibility to provide loyal and faithful service to an employer is called into question if he or she is "moonlighting", particularly for a competing business.

- Employers should recognise that low-paid workers may see moonlighting as a way of supplementing their income.

- Information which an employee receives or possesses in connection with his or her job, is held on trust for the employer, and should not be disclosed to a third party.

- Workplace affairs, particularly between people of differing seniority within an organisation, can cause friction with colleagues and accusations of favouritism.

- It is important for employers to maintain some overall standards at office parties, particularly those held off the premises. Management must spell out clearly to staff the types of behaviour that will not be tolerated.

- An employer is reasonable in expecting employees to move with the times and adapt to new working practices and techniques.

- Many employers prohibit gambling on the premises — even card games — because of the tensions it can cause between staff.

- Insolence by an employee can be viewed as gross misconduct, especially if it takes place in public or could cause commercial harm to the business.

- Employers do not have an inherent right to forcibly detain or search their staff.

- Employers owe a duty of care to their staff in protecting them from foreseeable violence, either from colleagues, customers or members of the public.

Useful Reading

The Suzy Lamplugh Trust is a national charity which promotes personal safety and produces a range of materials covering workplace violence.
14 East Sheen Avenue
London SW14 8AS

The Health and Safety Executive publishes a guide *Preventing Violence to Retail Staff* (HS(G) 133).

Compass Vision Ltd (Tel: 0141-775 1482) have produced two videos aimed at reducing the effect of violent workplace incidents.

8 Incapability

Introduction

Dealing with incompetent staff who seem incapable of performing the job they are employed to do is one of the most difficult, yet crucial, management responsibilities. An employer's business success depends on an efficient workforce all operating to certain minimum levels of performance. One employee's sub-standard contribution can minimise the benefits achieved by the rest of the staff.

One way of minimising the risk of being saddled with incompetent staff is to follow a rigorous recruitment and selection procedure. Ideally, this will weed out those applicants who are unsuitable according to the employer's own objective selection criteria, leaving those who appear to be the most competent and likely to succeed in the job. Unfortunately, as all those who are involved in personnel work know only too well, there is no guarantee that the successful candidate will perform up to standard *in practice*, so it is not uncommon for managers to have to wrestle with problems of poor job performance. Indeed, problems concerning standards of work can equally crop up in relation to existing, and possibly long-serving, staff.

An employee is under a duty to obey the lawful and reasonable orders of his or her employer and to carry them out to the best of their ability. An incompetent employee can cause lasting damage to the reputation of a business and the sooner management deal with a performance problem the better. There can be many explanations for sub-standard work by an employee and an employer should investigate the circumstances in relation to each individual. Ultimately it may be necessary to dismiss an employee who is incompetent and this is one of the potentially fair grounds of dismissal under s.98 of the **Employment Rights Act 1996** (ERA). However, dismissal should be seen as a last resort and an employee should normally be given every opportunity to improve first.

Incapability can arise either through incompetence or incapacity due to ill-health. Under s.98(3) of the ERA "capability" is assessed "by reference to skill, aptitude, health or any other physical or mental quality". The employer is in the best position to judge whether a particular employee's work performance is below standard and it is not the role of a tribunal to substitute its own view on what it considers are acceptable standards of work. It was stated in *Taylor v Alidair* [1978] IRLR 82, that "whenever a man is dismissed for incapacity or incompetence it is sufficient that the employer honestly believes on reasonable grounds that the man is incapable and incompetent. It is not necessary for the employer to prove that he is in fact incapable or incompetent". An employer has to be able to show objective evidence of the employee's incompetence in order to demonstrate that they held a reasonable belief.

Evidence of Incompetence

Evidence of the employee's incompetence could be provided in a variety of ways. Tangible proof of incompetence is best demonstrated by the employee's clearly unacceptable job performance, such as in *Lowndes v Specialist Heavy Engineering Ltd* [1976] IRLR 246, where the employee was held to have been fairly dismissed following a series of five serious and costly errors. Of course, it would be open to an employee to show that such mistakes as were made were caused by the lack of proper training given to him by his employer. In *Davison v Kent Meters Ltd* [1975] IRLR 145, an employee who assembled 471 out of 500 components in the wrong sequence was held to have been unfairly dismissed because she had not received the necessary training and supervision from management.

Where direct evidence of incompetence is not available, the views of the individual's manager or other senior colleagues can be significant. For instance, in *Cook v Thomas Linnell & Sons Ltd* [1977] IRLR 132, a manager was held to have been fairly dismissed when senior management lost confidence in him after a fall-off in trade. In his judgment, Phillips J said, "when responsible employers have genuinely come to the conclusion over a reasonable period of time that a manager is incompetent we think that it is some evidence that he is incompetent."

Similarly, dissatisfaction from other members of staff can be good evidence of professional incompetence, as in *Hooper v Feedex Ltd* [1974] IRLR 99, in which it was held to be fair to dismiss an employee who patently lacked the necessary skills to manage his unit and created such an unhappy atmosphere that several staff refused to work under him.

In *A J Dunning & Sons (Shopfitters) Ltd v Jacomb* [1973] IRLR 206, it was held to be fair to dismiss a contracts manager occupying a responsible position when his inability to get on with clients led to them making complaints against him and this in turn adversely affected the firm's business. He was found to have a "constitutional inability" to change his attitude towards these clients even though he was aware of the difficulties that he was causing.

Does the Employee Know What is Expected of Him?

The ACAS advisory handbook recommends that employers are guided by the following principles in respect of new staff.

- The standard of work required should be explained and employees left in no doubt about what is expected of them. Special attention should be paid to ensuring that standards are understood by employees whose English is limited and by young persons with little experience of working life.

- Where job descriptions are prepared they should accurately convey the main purpose and scope of each job and the tasks involved.
- Employees should be made aware of the conditions which are attached to any probation period.
- The consequences of any failure to meet the required standards should be explained.
- Where an employee is promoted, the consequences of failing to make the grade in the new job should be explained.

It is vital that an employee knows the standard of performance that is required in his or her job and every effort should be made by the employer to equip him or her with this knowledge. This could be done, for instance, by reference to the achievement of certain sales levels, production targets being hit or the securing of a specified number of new client introductions. Where there are no express performance indicators, it becomes even more important to appraise the employee at regular intervals in order to review work performance and provide feedback, particularly where there are management concerns about the employee's work.

Allowing an employee to continue to work to low standards sets new norms and suggests that nothing is amiss, making it all the more difficult to take remedial action later. Employers should also be wary of the dangers of giving an employee a glowing appraisal of his or her capabilities one day and accusing him or her of incompetence the next. The same problem can arise where an employee is dismissed for incompetence and is supplied with a favourable reference conveying a very different picture of his or her capabilities and performance, as in *Castledine v Rothwell Engineering* [1973] IRLR 99.

How to Deal With Poor Performance Problems

The ACAS advisory handbook provides the following guidelines for employers in cases of poor performance.

- The employee should be asked for an explanation and the explanation checked.
- Where the reason is a lack of the required skills, the employee should, wherever practicable, be assisted through training and given reasonable time to reach the required standard of performance.
- Where, despite encouragement and assistance, the employee is unable to reach the required standard of performance, consideration should be given to finding suitable alternative work.
- Where alternative work is not available, the position should be explained to the employee before dismissal action is taken.
- An employee should not normally be dismissed because of poor performance unless warnings and a chance to improve have been given.
- If the main cause of poor performance is the changing nature of the job, employers should consider whether the situation may properly be treated as a redundancy matter rather than a capability or conduct issue.

Where an employee's work performance appears to be below standard, an employer needs to discuss this with the individual concerned and resist doing anything precipitately. The need to follow a reasonable procedure is considered paramount by tribunals. In *James v Waltham Holy Cross UDC* [1973] IRLR 202, it was stated that:

> *An employer should be very slow to dismiss upon the grounds that the employee is incapable of performing the work which he is employed to do without first telling the employee of the respects in which he is failing to do his job adequately, warning him of the possibility or likelihood of*

dismissal on this ground, and giving him an opportunity to improve his performance.

Clearly, if there are concerns about the performance of an employee, some form of appraisal of the individual needs to have been done by management. The ACAS advisory handbook *Discipline at Work* defines an appraisal system as "a systematic method of obtaining and analysing information to evaluate an employee's performance in a job and assess his or her training and development needs and potential for future promotion". A fair and objective appraisal of the employee can show up weaknesses and provide the employee with a course of action in order to improve. This may involve further training and supervision over a period of time but it can prevent the problem of the employee's job performance getting out of hand.

Warnings and a Chance to Improve

As a general rule, it is considered essential to warn an employee about his or her unsatisfactory job performance before taking action against him or her. Failure to warn can render a dismissal unfair. A warning can serve to bring an employee back from the brink and be a powerful motivator once criticisms have been drawn to his or her attention. In *Winterhalter Gastronom Ltd v Webb* [1973] IRLR 120, it was stated that:

There are many situations in which a man's apparent capabilities may be stretched when he knows what is being demanded of him; many do not know that they are capable of jumping the five-barred gate until the bull is close behind them.

A warning should fully outline what is expected from an employee, the timescale for achieving it and the consequences of failure to do so. An employee should be given a reasonable time to improve. How long this should last depends on the circumstances and will take into account such factors as the nature of the employee's job, his or her previous work performance standards and his or her length of service. In *Evans v George Galloway & Co.* [1974] IRLR 167, it was considered to be insufficient to afford an employee with six years' service only five weeks to improve and in *Siburn v Modern Telephones Ltd* [1976] IRLR 81, three years was thought appropriate for a salesman with nearly twenty years' satisfactory performance.

If an employee fails to improve despite receiving suitable warnings, dismissal is likely to be fair. In *Lewis Shops Group v Wiggins* [1973] IRLR 205, a shop manager was held to have been fairly dismissed because she failed to heed warnings to tidy up her shop and organise things more efficiently.

Warnings are especially relevant where senior employees are concerned and it was held in *McPhail v Gibson* [1976] IRLR 254, that they should be explicitly told to improve and if they did not, that their job is at risk.

Normally, evidence of a course of unsatisfactory job performance is required before an employer takes action against an employee. In exceptional cases, one single incident of serious incompetence might be sufficient to warrant dismissal. This could arise where the employee's level of performance leads to the employer losing confidence in the employee's ability to do the job involved and the consequences are too serious for the employer to take the risk of allowing the employee to continue. In *Taylor v Alidair Ltd* [1978] IRLR 82, a pilot was dismissed for being responsible for badly damaging his aircraft in the course of a faulty landing. The EAT stated:

> *In our judgment there are activities in which the degree of professional skill which must be required is so high, and the potential consequences of the smallest departure from that high standard are so serious, that one failure to perform in accordance with those standards is enough to justify dismissal. The passenger-carrying airline pilot, the scientist operating the nuclear reactor, the chemist in charge of*

research into the possible effects of, for example, thalidomide,
the driver of the Manchester to London express, the driver of
an articulated lorry full of sulphuric acid, are all in a
position in which one failure to maintain the proper
standards of professional skill can bring about a major
disaster.

In cases such as these warnings are inappropriate, although
in *ILEA v Lloyd* [1981] IRLR 394, the Court of Appeal decided
that the principle enunciated in *Taylor* should be restricted to
cases where safety was involved. However, where an
employee's careless incompetence results in serious damage
to his or her employer's business interests, it may also be
appropriate to dismiss without warning in exceptional cases.
For instance, in *Turner v Pleasurama Casinos Ltd* [1976] IRLR
151, it was held that it was fair to dismiss a gaming inspector
without warning him first where he had lamentably failed to
spot a fraud occurring under his own eyes. In *O'Hagan v
Firestone Tyre* [1974] IRLR 226, it was held to have been fair
to have dismissed an industrial relations officer without
having first warned him of the possibility of dismissal,
"where his incapability was irredeemable". The job required
"an understanding of human nature, sensitivity to human
problems and ability to inspire confidence" and he made
matters worse by his arrogant and obstructive manner
during negotiations.

Sometimes it is necessary for employees to adapt to new
work methods and they show themselves unable to change
and the prospects of them doing so in the future are nil. A
warning here would serve no useful purpose. In *Hindle v
Percival Boats* [1969] 1 All ER 836, an old-fashioned craftsman
was unable to embrace new techniques in order to work
with fibreglass instead of wood and was dismissed fairly for
incapability. Similarly, where an individual is determined to
go his or her own way, or will not admit that he or she is
performing badly, a warning may be unnecessary since it
would make no difference to him or her.

Probationary Employees

Employers who take employees on as probationers have a contractual duty to appraise and give guidance to them during their probationary period. According to *Post Office v Mughal* [1977] IRLR 178, this probably includes training, counselling and, where necessary, warnings, in order to bring any performance issues to the employee's attention. If a probationer is dismissed, he or she could bring a claim for breach of contract if the employer failed to comply with its own contractual disciplinary or performance procedures prior to dismissal.

Over-promoted Employees

Sometimes an employee gains promotion and is found to be unable to cope with the new responsibilities of the post. In such a situation, it could be unfair to dismiss the employee without having given him or her such training as is necessary to enable him or her to fulfil the new job, as occurred in *Burrows v Ace Caravan Co. (Hull) Ltd* [1972] IRLR 4. Equally, it is all the more difficult for an employer to justify a dismissal on the grounds that an employee is incompetent having just given him or her a vote of confidence by promoting him or her.

Lack of Qualifications

"Qualifications" are defined in s.98(3)b of the ERA as "any degree, diploma or other academic, technical or professional qualification relevant to the position" which the employee held. Sometimes an employee is engaged on the understanding that he or she attain certain qualifications, or pass an aptitude test by a prescribed date, to remain in employment. If he or she does not do so, dismissal can be fair on this ground providing the qualifications are a substantial element of the job.

Alternative Work

Where an employee is incapable of doing the work through incompetence, there is no duty to find him or her alternative work to do instead, although a large employer should at least consider whether there is another job within the organisation which could be offered as opposed to dismissal.

Incapability Due to Hazardous Pursuits

Just as insurers can take a view on the risk attaching to individuals who put themselves in risky situations, an employer who regards an individual as a "key person", or indeed, pays a premium on "key person" insurance, may question an employee's decision to regularly undertake a hazardous pursuit outside work. This is, of course a controversial area but an individual who, for instance, persisted in going hang-gliding every weekend and suffered repeated injuries as a result, could be warned that his or her particular personal lifestyle is bringing his or her job into jeopardy.

Fines for Incompetence

Where an employee causes loss to his or her employer's business interests through carelessness or inefficiency, it is possible to fine him or her by deduction from his or her wages. However, the ability of an employer to do so is regulated by Part II of the ERA. In essence, a deduction is not permitted in these circumstances unless it is authorised in advance by a relevant provision of the worker's contract, or where the worker has previously signified in writing his or her agreement or consent to the making of the deduction.

Typically, deductions have been common where shop assistants have short-falls in their till at the end of the day and the employer seeks to defray these losses as against its employee's wage. Special rules apply to deductions for cash shortages and stock deficiencies from workers in retail employment and they can only lose up to one-tenth of the gross amount of wages payable to them on any of their pay days. However, deductions can be rolled over to the following pay intervals indefinitely until the deficiency is made up and the 10% limit does not apply to their final pay day on termination.

Civil Action

If an employee causes damage or loss to his or her employer's property through negligence, there is nothing to prevent the employer suing him or her for damages in the civil courts to gain recompense. This can arise in addition to dismissal of the employee in question. In *Janata Bank v Ahmed* [1981] IRLR 457, the Court of Appeal held that a former bank manager was liable to compensate his former employers more than £30,000 for losses they incurred due to his negligence.

Dismissal on the Grounds of Ill-Health

The absence of an employee from work due to illness presents an employer with a problem which needs careful handling. There are a number of competing issues which need to be addressed when dealing with staff sickness and there can be difficulties ahead for the business if an employer either ignores the problem or acts in an unreasonable manner towards an employee. The commercial and operational requirements of the business are important but so too are the interests of the particular employee.

The incidence and resulting cost of staff absence is a considerable drain on organisations generally. According to a survey in July 1995 by the CBI, 175 million working days were lost over the year, being the equivalent to 8 days per employee per year. The cost to the economy overall was estimated at £16 billion. Clearly, it is sensible for an employer to have policies and procedures to minimise the level of staff absenteeism and to deal fairly with employees whose attendance at work is unsatisfactory.

Problems over staff absence can arise due to an employee's long-term illness or as a result of their short-term but persistent absences. It is important to distinguish between the two because the former can raise questions of capability, whereas the latter often indicates misconduct or unreliability and necessitates the use of the employer's disciplinary procedures.

Absence due to sickness is a potentially fair ground for dismissal under s.98(2)(a) of the ERA. This covers dismissal of an employee on the ground of his or her capability, which is defined in s.98(3)(a) by reference to the employee's "… skill, aptitude, health or any other physical or mental quality…"

Before considering the question of dismissal for sickness absence, an employer may argue that the employee's contract of employment has been *frustrated* in the legal sense. If this is the case, there is no dismissal by the employer because the contract has simply been ended as a result of unforeseen outside events which were not the fault of either party to the contract. Because this prevents the employee from bringing a claim for unfair dismissal, the courts are reluctant to concede that illness has frustrated a contract of employment. The case of *James v The Greytree Trust* [1996] IDS Brief 566, demonstrates the cautious approach tribunals are taking in relation to frustration. Here it was held that a four month period of sickness absence for an employee with eighteen years' service did not amount to frustration of her contract and that she had been dismissed for incapacity by her employer, which may or may not have been fair in the particular circumstances. Her employers had failed to take into account her long service, the fact that her contract provided for long periods of sickness absence and overall they had acted too hastily in viewing her contract as frustrated rather than adopting a proper procedure to investigate her long-term incapacity. Whether a contract is frustrated or not is a question of law for a tribunal to answer and not one for an individual employer.

In cases of long-term staff sickness absence, an employer has a duty to act fairly and to consider all the facts of the case before coming to a decision to dismiss. In *Spencer v Paragon Wallpapers Ltd* [1976] IRLR 373, it was said that:

> *every case depends on its own circumstances. The basic question which has to be determined in every case is whether, in all the circumstances, the employer can be expected to wait any longer, and, if so, how much longer?*

The factors which need to be weighed up by an employer are:

- the length of the employee's previous employment and his or her attendance record up until the present illness
- the nature of the employee's job and the position he or she occupies within the organisation
- the effect of the employee's continued absence on the employer's business and any need by the employer to engage a replacement worker
- the exact nature and length of the employee's illness and the prospects for his or her recovery
- the terms of the employee's contract of employment in relation to sickness absence, including any entitlement to company sick pay.

According to the decision in *East Lindsey District Council v Daubney* [1977] IRLR 181, an employer must be able to make an *informed* judgment about the absent employee's overall situation. This is achieved by proper enquiry and consultation. It is advisable to seek a medical report from the employee's doctor in order to obtain the true medical position and this should be fully discussed with the employee before coming to any decision about his or her future. Sometimes it is preferable for the company doctor to examine the employee and in the event of conflicting medical reports an independent doctor should be consulted.

Whichever doctors are involved, it is important to inform the employee of his or her statutory rights as regards access to his or her medical records and reports. It is significant to note that the decision whether or not to dismiss is ultimately not a medical one but a *management* one, medical evidence being simply one important factor in coming to a decision.

Where an employee is prevented by ill-health from doing his or her present job, an employer should consider offering any suitable alternative work, such as lighter duties, before moving to dismiss him or her. In *Taylorplan Catering (Scotland) Ltd v McInally* [1980] IRLR 53, it was stated that there was no *obligation* on an employer to create a new post specially for the employee. According to the decision in *London Fire & Civil Defence Authority v Betty* [1994] IRLR 384, the fact that the employee's illness was work-related is not a relevant factor when considering whether a dismissal for incapability was a fair one.

Where there is a contractual permanent health insurance scheme for employed staff, the High Court held recently in *Aspden v Webb's Poultry & Meat Group (Holdings) Ltd* [1996] IRLR 52, that there was an implied term that the employer could not dismiss for ill-health thereby depriving employees of the benefits of the health scheme. Dismissal for misconduct, such as malingering, was however possible.

Persistent short-term staff absenteeism can be more damaging to an employer's interests than isolated long-term absences. It can be treated as a disciplinary issue in which warnings are appropriate and the employee should be made aware that he or she is putting his or her job in jeopardy unless things improve over a prescribed period. Ultimately, the employee could be dismissed on the misconduct ground under s.98(2)(b) of the ERA because of unreliability or on the basis that the employee's persistent absences or poor attendance gave the employer "some other substantial reason" justifying the dismissal within s.98(1)(b) of the ERA.

In *International Sports Co. Ltd v Thomson* [1980] IRLR 340, it was stressed that in the case of persistent intermittent absences, a formal medical investigation "would rarely be fruitful because of the transient nature of the employee's symptoms and complaints". What is required is a fair review of the employee's attendance record and the reasons for it and the issuing of appropriate warnings after the employee has had the chance to state his or her case. A subsequent failure to improve is likely to be a sufficient reason to dismiss.

In *British Coal Corporation v Bowers* [1994] IDS Brief 541, the EAT held that in the case of persistent short-term absence for unconnected ailments, an employer is entitled to look at the employee's absenteeism *as a whole*. Furthermore, the EAT held that the ACAS Booklet *Discipline at Work* merely contained guidelines on absenteeism and was not a code of practice which employers had to follow rigidly.

Summary

- Sub-standard performance by one employee can minimise the benefits achieved by the rest of the staff.

- Problems with standards of work can occur in both new and existing staff.

- New staff may cite poor training as a reason for their incompetence.

- In order to dismiss for incapability, an employer must be able to show objective evidence of the employee's incompetence.

- Employees should be left in no doubt as to what is expected of them.

- Consult fully with the employee before coming to any final decisions. An under-performing employee should be asked for an explanation and given reasonable time to reach the required standard.

- In exceptional cases, one single incident of serious incompetence might warrant dismissal.

- A deduction from wages in order to make good a loss caused by an employee's incompetence is only permitted if authorised in advance by contract or written agreement.

- The extent and cost of staff absence places a considerable burden on businesses.

- Absence can be long-term or repeated short-term time off.

- An employee can be dismissed for prolonged absence but employers must act fairly and take into account a range of factors, including length of employment and previous attendance record.

- In cases of persistent, short-term absence, the matter can be treated as a disciplinary one. The employer should investigate and warn the employee that failure to improve attendance standards may lead to dismissal.

9   Smoking in the Workplace

Introduction

Although bans on individuals smoking in some industries, such as those involving food processing and explosives manufacture, have existed for many years, the period from 1993 to 1995 witnessed a significant increase in the incidence of employers, generally, introducing workplace no-smoking policies. A variety of recent surveys have confirmed that the vast majority of employers now operate some controls on smoking at work and the numbers doing so continue to rise each year.

A survey by Reed in 1994 found that 86% of employers operated some controls on workplace smoking and that 94% of employers with over 1000 employees either banned completely or restricted smoking at work. Of the employers who responded, 30% reported that they would rather hire non-smokers. These findings were broadly confirmed by the Institute of Business Ethics in 1995, whose research found that 92% of employers operated a smoking policy. In 1996, an IDS survey found that of those employers that maintained such a policy, two fifths operated a blanket ban on smoking at work.

In the continuing battle between various pressure groups and the Tobacco Industry, it has been estimated by Action on Smoking and Health (ASH) that up to 50 million working days are lost every year due to smoking-related illness, costing British industry as much as £3 billion. According to the British Medical Association, cigarettes are the greatest single cause of avoidable death and disability, contributing to 120,000 deaths a year. The Tobacco Advisory Council maintains that smokers contribute over £8 billion to the State in tobacco taxes every year. In certain situations there can be health and safety implications in permitting employees to smoke at work, such as in premises where flammable materials are present or where hygiene regulations will be contravened where foodstuffs are prepared. An employer may also face potential legal claims for compensation from employees who are victims of passive smoking (see page 162).

Why Have a Smoking Policy?

There are a number of interrelated reasons why employers have decided to implement workplace rules governing smoking, despite the fact that measures which restrict personal freedoms are inevitably controversial and can, in themselves, cause disruption to a business through staff dissent. The motivating factors behind some employers' decisions to introduce workplace smoking policies can be seen in the following perceptions:

- to create a cleaner and healthier working environment for staff
- as an aid to recruitment of staff
- to increase workplace efficiency and output
- to reduce staff sickness absence due to having a fitter workforce
- to reduce the costs of premises' maintenance and redecoration
- to decrease insurance premiums, as a result of the reduced fire risk
- to decrease the likelihood of a successful civil claim against the employer by passive smokers
- to create a better environment for existing and potential customers and clients
- to present a better corporate image to the public
- to satisfy the public's expectation of the particular organisation

- to demonstrate good practice and further the Government's "Health of the Nation" campaign
- to comply with specific statutory health and safety rules
- to fulfill the employer's common law duty of care towards its staff
- to improve staff interrelationships
- to reduce management time in handling conflicts and complaints at work.

Some employers fear that the introduction of workplace smoking policies can have some potential disadvantages. The following may result:
- a lack of morale in smokers
- a worsening of industrial relations
- a disincentive for some potential employees
- the possibility of loss of workers unable to comply with the policy
- an increase in stress among smokers
- a potentially increased fire risk caused by smoking in unauthorised areas
- more attention may be paid to avoiding detection than properly extinguishing the cigarette
- the cost of providing alternative facilities for smokers
- if smokers are forced to smoke off the premises, a poor public image can be created
- staff may have to cope with unpleasant scenes when enforcing the policy against outsiders
- the loss of valuable staff time when smokers leave to have a cigarette
- difficulties involved in policing such a policy and responding to any breaches by staff.

Legal Impetus

Employers without policies on workplace smoking face the very real possibility of legal action being taken against them on a variety of fronts. Employees who have to work on a daily basis in close proximity to others who smoke are potential passive smoking victims. The involuntary inhalation of tobacco fumes is said to be harmful to health, although the tobacco industry disputes this. An employer owes a duty of care to staff to ensure that they work in a safe environment and to take measures to achieve this. If an employee could prove that his or her health has suffered because of his or her exposure to tobacco smoke at work, civil claims for damages might succeed.

As yet, however, no claimant in the UK has been awarded compensation by a court for being the victim of passive smoking but there have been several out-of-court settlements made by employers. Stockport Borough Council have twice made payments in order to settle claims by employees who claimed that the Council was liable for their ill-health due to there being no workplace smoking policy in operation and a failure by their employers to respond to their repeated complaints about proper ventilation. Although the Council denied responsibility in both cases, it paid Ms Bland £15,000 in 1993 and Ms Roe £25,000 in 1995.

Claims by passive smokers are based on the principles of common law negligence. The employer owes a duty of care to the employee, the employer has failed to discharge that duty by taking such steps as are reasonable and the employee has suffered loss or damage as a direct result. Proving *all* of these necessary factors is difficult for a claimant. However, by continuing to allow smoking at work in an uncontrolled way, and in the light of all the current medical thinking and Health and Safety Executive advice, employers would be in danger of failing to show that they have properly discharged their duty of care. This is especially so because in 1990 it was held in *Clay v The Adjudication Officer* (Case No. 2/11/1935) that an employee who was an asthma sufferer had suffered an industrial injury by her exposure to workplace tobacco smoke, so the risks are well-known. The only real obstacle then for a claimant to overcome is that of proving the connection between his or her ill-health and the workplace. Here, an employer might be able to show that the employee's condition was caused, or substantially contributed to, by non-workplace factors, such as living with a smoker, or frequenting places with smoky atmospheres, such as pubs.

Criminal Dimension

By virtue s.2(1) of the **Health and Safety at Work, etc Act 1974** (HSWA), an employer is under a statutory duty to "ensure, so far as is reasonably practicable, the health, safety and welfare of all his employees". Under s.2(2)(e), an employer must provide and maintain for employees a working environment which is, "so far as is reasonably practicable, safe and without risks to health, and adequate as regards facilities and arrangements for their welfare at work". An employer who fails to carry out its duties under the HSWA is guilty of a criminal offence. Therefore, employers who don't take preventative action to stop passive smoking could ultimately be prosecuted by Health and Safety Inspectors, although as yet, there have been no prosecutions in respect of workplace smoking.

Employees, while at work, are also placed under a duty by s.7 of the HSWA to "take reasonable care for the health and safety of himself and of other persons who may be affected by his act or omissions…". This compulsory concern for others could be compromised where an employee breaches a workplace smoking policy.

Rest Areas

Since 1 January 1996, as a result of the **Workplace (Health, Safety and Welfare) Regulations 1992**, employers who choose to provide rest areas or rooms for their staff at work are bound to ensure that such places are smoke-free. The Regulations, which apply to all workplaces, effectively mean that there must be separate rest facilities for smokers and non-smokers, failing which there must be a total ban on smoking in all rest areas and rooms. In a 1996 IRS survey, nearly half of employers provided a designated staff smoking room, usually with regulated access.

It is possible to insist that potential new recruits agree to abide by the in-house smoking policy and to incorporate it into their initial contracts of employment. This can be achieved by an express term in the contract which makes compliance with the employer's smoking policy mandatory. The code itself must be properly communicated to the staff and should be distributed to new employees on their induction, or first day of work.

How to Introduce a Policy

The introduction of a policy on smoking at work raises a combination of managerial and legal issues. An employer has an inherent right to manage the staff and to lay down rules relating to staff conduct and behaviour. It was said by the EAT in *Dryden v Greater Glasgow Health Board* [1992] IRLR 469 that there:

> can be no doubt that an employer is entitled to make rules for the conduct of employees in their place of work, as he is entitled to give lawful orders, within the scope of the contract; nor can there be any doubt, in our view, that once it has been held that there is no implied right in the contract which entitled the employee to facilities for smoking, a rule against smoking is, in itself, a lawful rule.

Consultation

Before implementing a policy regulating smoking, an employer should carry out a consultation exercise among staff to gauge attitudes. There should also be an assessment of the numbers of smokers and non-smokers that are employed and where they work in the organisation. The physical layout of the premises is an important factor and also whether there is open-plan or shared office working.

Consultation should also look into staff attitudes to smoking at work and whether there is a strong feeling that it should be regulated and, if so, how this should be done. The views of smokers should also be carefully noted because an employer has a duty towards all of its workforce. Consultation can take a variety of forms, including meetings, questionnaires, ballots, surveys and discussions with trade unions, workplace representatives and staff councils.

Varieties of Smoking Policy

Policies may be formal or informal. Informal policies rely heavily on the co-operation and goodwill of the staff concerned and are unlikely to have any method of enforcement. Voluntary policies can be used as a first step and, if successful, obviate the need for the introduction of more formal ones. The vast majority of employers, however, have formal, written policies on smoking at work. These operate regardless of staff consent and will contain enforcement mechanisms.

Having analysed the available feedback, an employer who concludes that regulation is necessary must decide on the degree of restriction. There are a number of possibilities. At one end of the scale there is a complete ban on smoking on the employer's premises, as is the norm in health care organisations and in the food industry. Alternatively, smoking might be permitted on the premises but only in designated smoking areas, such as smoking rooms. If this option is preferred, the question of access to such areas needs to be addressed. Much resentment from non-smokers can be built up if smokers are allowed to leave their work stations whenever they please to have a cigarette. According to the research group Lifestyle at Work, smokers who take cigarette breaks are working one day a week less than their non-smoking colleagues because a nine-a-day smoker who takes ten minutes on a cigarette break wastes seven and a half hours of company time each week. Furthermore, staff in a smoking room can be seen as unapproachable by their colleagues while they are there. Adequate means of ventilation is a priority.

Some organisations only limit smoking in shared workplaces and permit it where an employee has his or her own individual office. The difficulty here is that since it is more likely that senior staff have their own offices, smoking can become a perk of senior management, which is both divisive and unfair.

The *scope* of a smoking policy also needs to be addressed. Will it apply to outsiders on the premises and, if so, what communication and enforcement measures will be adopted? Extending a smoking ban to staff vehicles being used on company business and to staff whose work takes them off the premises can be justified on the basis of a detrimental public image, although enforcement problems can arise.

Implementation

Having devised a suitable policy, an employer should give the staff at least twelve weeks' advance notice of its introduction. All the staff should be informed verbally and in writing. The more publicity the better and good staff communications are essential on an issue as sensitive as this. It is considered good practice to phase in a new smoking policy before it becomes fully operational. Typically, employers do this over a three-month period (or more).

Dealing with Breaches of the Policy

If non-compliance with a smoking policy is treated by the employer as a disciplinary matter, it is imperative that fair disciplinary procedures are followed. This means that there must be a proper investigation into the facts of the case and a hearing at which the employer has the right to answer the charges. An employee should be permitted representation by a colleague or workplace representatives and there should be a route of appeal against any disciplinary sanction that is imposed.

An employer must act consistently when handling any disciplinary matter, so it must be even-handed between employees when tackling alleged breaches of a smoking code. This principle applies to the subsequent imposition of any disciplinary penalties as well as to the initiation of disciplinary investigations against individual members of staff.

Employees with at least two years' continuous service with their employers could claim that they have been unfairly dismissed, or they might resign and claim constructive dismissal in response to their employer's actions in disciplining them as they did.

In *Upton and Jones v Scotia Barry Foods* (COIT 19187/87), the employer had a no-smoking policy but had permitted breaches of it in the past due to "extenuating circumstances". Two employees found smoking were dismissed. This was held to be unfair dismissal because the employees had been given no opportunity to defend themselves and there was also *prima facie* evidence of inconsistent treatment between employees at the company.

In *Watson v Cooke, Webb & Holton (Insurance Brokers) Ltd* (COIT 13852/54), an industrial tribunal held the introduction of a smoking ban without prior notice to an employee who smoked, and without considering any practical alternatives to help her, was unfair.

Similarly, in *Wright v Ladbroke Racing Ltd* (COIT 54266/91), a long-serving employee with an excellent work record was held to have been unfairly dismissed for breaching the company's smoking ban in the counter area of its betting shops. Although the policy had been properly introduced with three months' advance notice to staff, the employer was held to have acted too precipitately in beginning disciplinary proceedings against the employee immediately the ban came into effect. In view of this employee's service and work record, and her particular opposition to the ban being introduced, the tribunal felt that her employers should have continued their efforts to find a solution to the problem for at least a further month before taking action against her.

In *Pascoe v C V James t/a Chris James* (COIT 2558/191), the employer had a policy that employees couldn't smoke in the workplace, in company vehicles and on customers' premises. A landscape gardener was held to have been unfairly dismissed for smoking in a customer's kitchen, before starting work and with the customer's consent. The tribunal felt the sanction of dismissal to be too excessive, despite the existence of the employer's code.

In *Marks & Spencer plc v O'Connell* [1996] IDS Brief 579, the EAT held that the employer had acted unreasonably by automatically dismissing the employee for smoking on duty in breach of staff regulations because they had failed to take into account the individual circumstances of the case. The company staff regulations permitted smoking by employees only in the staff lounge and in the roof garden at stated times. Smoking is prohibited in all other places and at all other times. Contravention of the regulations by staff was stated to result in summary dismissal. Mr O'Connell was called upon to work a 12-hour night shift to keep outsiders off the premises while outside contractors installed new escalators inside one of the company's stores. On being observed smoking on the tiled area outside the store by a security surveillance officer, he was summarily dismissed. This was upheld as an unfair dismissal by the EAT for the following reasons.

1. The contractors and members of the public had been smoking on the tiled area and in the immediate vicinity of the front of the store on the night in question.

2. Mr O'Connell had little scope for a work break during his duties on that night.
3. This was an isolated incident by Mr O'Connell which had occurred in exceptional circumstances.
4. The company's rules on smoking were a partial, rather than a total, ban specifically designed to prevent fire hazards. Mr O'Connell's behaviour did not amount to a fire hazard since it occurred outside and where the company premises adjoined the public footpath.

However, if an employee contravenes an express ban on smoking, properly introduced and communicated to staff, spelling out the serious consequences for breach, dismissal is likely to be fair. Accordingly, in *Martin v Selective Print Ltd* (COIT 1859/64) the tribunal held it was fair to dismiss an employee for smoking in a greeting cards factory and in *O'Hara v Avana Bakeries* (COIT 1766/54) a bakery worker who was involved in the manufacture of fresh food was held to have been fairly dismissed for smoking in defiance of a ban. In *Cruz-Suarez v MBM Technology Ltd* (COIT 3489/95), it was held to have been fair to dismiss an employee who defied a "no smoking on the premises" rule by going into the roof space of the building where combustible materials were stored.

Help and Assistance for Smokers

Employers must accept that in the UK 17 million people smoke and a significant proportion of these will be in employment and thereby affected by the introduction of a smoking policy. It is unrealistic to expect that smokers will be able to give up the habit simply because a workplace ban is imposed. Nicotine is a powerfully addictive drug, as addictive as heroin, and research shows that 70% of smokers have tried to stop at least twice. In March 1997, the American tobacco company Liggett Group for the first time admitted that cigarettes were addictive and caused a range of illnesses including cancer.

Smoking calms the nerves, relaxes the muscles and attenuates the appetite. Individuals who stop smoking may suffer from poor concentration, bad temper and a craving for sweet foods. Clearly, a caring employer will respect their position and offer support, advice and assistance. There are a range of possible support mechanisms, including the following:

- allowing time-off to attend "stop smoking" classes and clinics, such as those organised by the local health education authority
- encouraging staff to accept support and encouragement from the occupational health staff
- establishing self-help groups at work
- issuing practical hints on how to stop smoking
- providing nicotine patches
- giving staff access to trained counsellors
- providing hypnotherapy, acupuncture or aromatherapy treatment
- encouraging staff to gain advice and information from local GPs
- giving interest-free loans to seek treatment.

Monitoring the Policy

Whenever a policy is introduced it should be reviewed on a regular basis through consultation with staff. This is important in order to judge its effectiveness against stated objectives and, where necessary, modifications can then be made. A review cycle should be established, the first being after an interval of six months and thereafter every year.

Summary

- There are advantages and disadvantages in implementing a policy on smoking in the workplace.

- The vast majority of employers now have such a policy.

- Employers without workplace smoking policies risk legal action from non-smoking employees who may believe themselves to be the victims of passive smoking.

- When considering the case for passive smoking, the employee's home life and social habits, such as frequenting smoky pubs, will be taken into account.

- Rest areas for staff must be smoke-free, or separate facilities provided for smokers and non-smokers.

- Consultation should take place with all staff prior to implementing a policy on smoking.

- Employers implementing a policy should offer practical support, advice and assistance to staff to help them comply.

Useful Reading

Passive Smoking at Work is available from:
HSE Information Centre
Broad Lane
Sheffield S3 7HQ
Tel: 0114 278 2345

A workplace smoking policy: how to plan and introduce a policy to control smoking in the workplace is available from:
Health Education Authority
Hamilton House
Mableton Place
London WC1H 9TX
Tel: 0171-383 3833

Implementing a Smoking Policy (Checklist 063) is available from:
Institute of Management
Cottingham Road
Corby
Northants NN17 1TT
Tel: 01536 204222

10 Ageism

Introduction

Ageism involves treating individuals in a particular way because of their age. In the context of employment, this can mean the creation of a barrier by an employer at the point of recruitment, raising an obstacle to the training and promotion prospects of certain staff and an increased likelihood of them being selected for redundancy. Ageism typically disadvantages the old but the young too can suffer in the job market.

Currently, there are no laws in the UK against ageism. Treating a person less favourably than another amounts to discrimination but it is only unlawful if that discrimination is based on certain grounds, such as sex, race or disability. In several other countries, such as the United States, France, Canada and Australia, laws have been passed to prohibit age discrimination, although it is open to question how successful these laws have been in eliminating the problem in these countries.

There has been much talk in the UK about bringing in a statute to outlaw ageism and there appears to be significant popular support for this, including from employers. The Government favours a voluntary rather than mandatory code of behaviour and, in February 1997, published research by BMRB International which showed that nearly 60% of employers thought that a law would not work in practice and therefore opposed legislation. Recent parliamentary initiatives have been by way of Private Members' Bills and to date all have foundered, the most recent being the **Employment (Upper Age Limits in Advertising) Bill**. It is, however, Labour Party policy to bring in legislation to ban ageism in the employment field.

The problems posed by ageism are unlikely to evaporate because the UK has an ageing workforce and will continue to do so for some time to come. The official statistics and predictions highlight the future demographic trends of the UK population and these indicate that the problems concerned with ageism are something which employers will be faced with well into the next century.

Statistics

The following statistics show the extent to which the employment field will be affected by issues of age.

- By the year 2000 one-third of the workforce will be aged over 40.
- By the year 2006 24% of the workforce will be aged over 50 as compared with 21% in 1995.
- By the year 2010 the over-50s' group will be bigger than the 15–44 age group.
- By the year 2021 half of the population will be aged over 50.
- By the year 2026 30% of the people aged over 16 will be of pensionable age.
- By the year 2099 the 50–65 age group will be growing at more than double the rate of the rest of the population.
- Today, only 60% of men in the 55–64 age category are in work compared to 90% in the mid-1970s.
- Less than two-thirds of people aged over 50 years are economically active compared to 80% in the 35–49 age group.
- According to a Gallup poll, 83% of those who are unemployed in the 45 years and over age group believe that their age will hamper their efforts to find another job and 70% think that they will never work again.
- A survey by Austin Knight Research and the Employers Forum on Age found that one in four employees had suffered from ageism during their working careers and

over half of them because they were too young. The peak ages at which age discrimination is most likely to hit men is around 18 years and 50 years, while for women the ages were found to be 21 years and 40 years. Almost 80% of 2000 employees in the survey favoured legislation against age discrimination. Only one third of those who reported age discrimination took any action about it and only one sixth made an informal complaint. One in six employees simply moved on to another organisation.

- A joint report by the Institute of Management and Manchester Metropolitan University found that 85% of managers felt that employers should treat age as an equal opportunities issue.

- The New Earnings Survey found that in 1995, full-time earnings peaked for men when they were in the 40–49 age bracket, while for women it was in the 30–39 year age bracket.

- According to the Department for Education and Employment (DfEE), evidence suggests that 40% of employers practice age discrimination and one quarter of unemployment among men and women in the 50–59 age group is over three years' duration.

- Age Concern research found that more than 80% of workers aged 50 or over felt that they had been turned down for a job because of their age.

- A survey of the Institute of Employment Consultants' members in 1994 found up to 60% of job vacancies contained an age-related restriction and 74% of employers actively recruiting sought candidates in the 21–30 age range.

- The 1994 Manchester Metropolitan University survey revealed that up to 37% of personnel managers admit to using age limits when recruiting.

- Research by Barkers Human Resources indicated that the incidence of adverts containing age barriers is falling and in 1995 stood at 11%.

In What Circumstances Can Age Requirements in Jobs be Unlawful in the UK?

Where an employer advertises a job which contains a lower age requirement, such as 18 to 30, this can be challenged on the basis that it constitutes indirect sex discrimination. An example of this occurred in *Price v Civil Service Commission* [1977] IRLR 291, in which the EAT held that the stipulation that applicants for the post of executive officer between the ages of 17 and 28 was prima facie discriminatory. The proportion of women who could comply with the requirement in practice was less than the proportion of men who could do so because less women were in the job market during this period due to family commitments. An employer who includes such an age requirement would have to justify the need for it in relation to its business and there can be few circumstances where the defence will be able to succeed.

Where the complaint is that an employer specifies an upper age limit for a job, such as 50 years, it is not possible to argue that it amounts to indirect sex discrimination because the requirement affects potential job applicants of both sexes equally.

Using age as the *sole* instrument in redundancy selection was held to be unlawful by an industrial tribunal in *Walker, Nolan & Kiddy v Carbodies Ltd* (1994) (unreported), in which three men in their early sixties were awarded a total of £41,163 compensation having been selected for dismissal without reference to their respective skills, experience and length of service. Similarly, in *Todd & Tuck v Filtrona Ltd* (1996) (unreported), two cigarette factory workers in their early sixties who were sacked because their advancing years did not fit their company's younger age profile received £30,000 in settlement of their unfair dismissal claim.

Employer Attitudes towards Older Workers

Those employers who perpetuate ageist policies do so out of misguided prejudice and a host of misconceptions about older workers. In the DfEE's booklet *Age Works*, examples are given of some typical employer attitudes towards older workers:

- their skills will be outdated
- it's harder to train older people
- there's less of a payback period on training
- they're less fit and healthy
- they're not flexible
- they'll want more money
- we always have young secretaries
- we need to keep the number of applicants down
- we had an older person once who was hopeless
- they might be unwilling to work for a younger person.

The Benefits of Older Workers

During the past few years, there has been a concerted effort by the Government and a number of organisations to dispel some of the myths and generalisations highlighted above. The message has been to appoint staff on merit regardless of their age and to stress the business case for doing so.

One of the benefits of employing older workers is that they provide greater continuity of service. This is because workers in their twenties have a turnover rate four times higher than older workers. This can be costly for a large organisation, such as WH Smith, where a 1% turnover in staff costs the company £800,000 a year. Other benefits of employing older workers are said to be that they:

- can generate increased customer satisfaction for many organisations
- result in a balanced workforce for an employer and can solve skill shortages

- are able to use their greater experience and judgment
- are more confident, loyal, dedicated and committed, with a stronger work ethic
- are able to learn new skills at least as quickly as younger workers
- spend less time off sick, especially over short periods and are thus more reliable
- present fewer disciplinary problems to management and have a high degree of honesty
- have lower accident rates
- are better at working in teams and are less impulsive than younger workers.

What Can Employers do to Reduce Ageism?

There are a range of measures which can be adopted by employers in an effort to combat ageism at work. The DfEE guidance booklet *Getting On* suggests that there are five steps to effective action:
- drop age bars
- select on ability
- welcome older applicants
- offer flexible working
- invest in all your workers, regardless of age.

A survey in 1995 by Barkers Human Resources indicates that some progress is being made in relation to the dropping of age bars, with only 11% of adverts now containing age barriers. In 1996, People Management magazine began a policy of refusing to take job adverts which contain numerical age limits. The recruitment industry has also taken the initiative by signing a policy declaration in 1996. Sixty three agencies, representing 90% of the recruitment advertising market and £400 million worth of business annually, pledged themselves to the following four-point code.

1. Avoid initiating the inclusion of age limits in adverts they prepare.
2. Question clients' requests to include age limits.
3. Seek to include an explanation of limits in adverts.
4. Do not automatically exclude applicants whose ages fall outside the limit.

Attitudes generally seem to be changing and a report by the Institute of Management found that 85% of managers felt that employers should treat age as an equal opportunities issue.

Initiatives which employers can take are:

– to take the date of birth out of application forms
– to look beyond an applicant's qualifications to consider their experience, skills, maturity, commitment and knowledge
– to use aptitude tests as a selection tool
– to avoid negative stereotypes
– to develop realistic job descriptions.

The Institute of Management recommend that employers:

– review their recruitment and selection procedures for objectivity
– apply a developmentally led approach to ensure that all employees maintain skills, have training and mid-career counselling to identify their development needs and preferences
– examine the scope for older managers and workers to act as formal or informal mentors to less experienced staff
– consider the possibility of flexible transition to retirement in the context of pensions
– examine the potential for developing a flexible "skill bank" of retired, or early retired, employees to be used on a consultancy basis or in order to manage peak periods of demand
– ensure that their organisations clearly state their antipathy towards any form of discrimination, including

on the grounds of age and to incorporate age into their equal opportunities policies.

The Institute of Personnel & Development recommends that employers:

- examine their use of advertising, application forms and interviews to ensure that they are not age-biased
- ensure that an individual's age is not used in order to make judgments about their abilities or fitness and where a judgment is required, consult an occupational health or medical practitioner
- ensure that pay and terms and conditions are not based on age-related criteria but reflect individual standards of job performance and the value of the individual's contribution to overall objectives
- ensure that particular age groups are not automatically excluded from training and development programmes, since this is inefficient
- consider the future needs for knowledge, skills and competencies when making staff redundant
- consider alternatives to redundancy, such as shorter hours, part-time working, and secondments
- consider giving older men and women the opportunity to have phased retirement, flexible working, to work beyond the normal retirement age, or on a self-employed basis, or in the voluntary sector and to mentor other employees.

Summary

- Ageism is not illegal in the UK except if it can be shown to be discrimination based on sex, race or disability.

- UK employers will increasingly have to deal with an ageing workforce because of demographic trends.

- Using age as the sole instrument in redundancy selection can be unlawful.

- Younger workers are likely to have a higher turnover rate than older ones.

- Employers who practice age discrimination will miss out on a range of benefits which can be derived from employing older workers.

Where to Find Help

The Employers Forum on Age (ERA)
Astral House
1268 London Road
London SW16 4ER

The Third Age Challenge Trust
Anglia House
115 Cambridge Road
Swindon SW1 5PL

Useful Reading

Age Works (PL991) and *Too Old..who says?* (PL974) and *Getting On* (PL949) are available from:

Department for Education and Employment
Cambertown Ltd
Unit 8
Goldthorpe Industrial Estate
Goldthorpe
Rotherham S63 9BL
Tel: 01709 888688

Evaluation of the campaign for older workers is available from:
BMRB International, commissioned by
Department for Education and Employment
HMSO Bookshops
Tel: 0171-873 9090

Useful Addresses

Harassment

Commission for Racial Equality
Elliot House
10–12 Allington Street
London SW1E 5EH
Tel: 0171-828 7022

Equal Opportunities Commission
Overseas House
Quay Street
Manchester M3 3HN
Tel: 0161-833 9244

Advisory, Conciliation and Arbitration Service
Head Office
Brandon House
180 Borough High Street
London SE1 1LW
Tel: 0171-210 3000

Drugs and Alcohol

Al Anon
61 Great Dover Street
London SE1 4YF
Tel: 0171-403 0888

Alcoholics Anonymous
PO Box 1
Stonebow House
Stonebow
York YO1 2NJ
Tel: 01904 644026

Alcohol Concern
Waterbridge House
32–36 Loman Street
London SE1 OEE
Tel: 0171-928 7377

Institute of Alcohol Studies
Alliance House
Caxton Street
London SW1M OQS
Tel: 0171-222 5880

Health Education Authority
Hamilton House
Mableton Place
London WC1H 9TX
Tel: 0171-383 3833

Turning Point
9–12 Long Lane
London EC1A 9HA
Tel: 0171-702 2300

Standing Conference on Drug Abuse
Waterbridge House
32–36 Loman Street
London SE1 OEE
Tel: 0171-928 9500

National Drugs Helpline
Tel: 0800 776600

AIDS

The Terrence Higgins Trust
52/54 Gray's Inn Road
London WC1X 8JU
Tel: 0171-831 0330

Employers' Advisory Service on AIDS and HIV
PO Box HP346
Leeds LS6 1UL
Tel: 0113 294 1212

National AIDS Helpline
Tel: 0800 567 123

National AIDS Trust
New City Cloisters
188–196 Old Street
London EC1V 9FR
Tel: 0171-814 6767
(subscriptions to the Advisory Service £100 per annum)

Foreign and Commonwealth Office
Travel Enquiries Unit
Tel: 0171-270 4129

ACET
Training and Advice on the Spread of HIV/AIDS
PO Box 3693
London SW15 2BQ
Tel: 0181-780 0400

Stress

The Industrial Society
48 Bryanston Square
London W1H 7LN
Tel: 0171-262 2401

British Association of Counselling
Eastlands Court
St. Peter's Road
Rugby CV21 3QP

The Institute of Management
Cottingham Road
Corby
Northants NN17 1TT
Tel: 01536 204222

Disability

Employers' Forum on Disability
Nutmeg House
60 Gainsford Street
London SE1 2NY
Tel: 0171-403 3020

Smoking

Quitline
Tel: 0171-487 3000

Action on Smoking and Health (ASH)
16 Fitzharding Street
London W1H 9PL
Tel: 0171-224 0743

FOREST
(Freedom Organisation for the Right to Enjoy Smoking Tobacco)
2 Grosvenor Gardens
London SW1W ODH
Tel: 0171-823 6550

HSE Information Centre
Broad Lane
Sheffield S3 7HQ
Tel: 0114 289 2345

Health and Safety Executive
Rose Court
2 Southwark Bridge
London SE1 9HS
Tel: 0171-717 6000

QUIT
Victory House
170 Tottenham Court Road
London W1P OHA
Tel: 0171-388 5775

British Lung Foundation
8 Peterborough Mews
London SW6 3BL
Tel: 0171-371 7704

Ageism

Advisory Group on Older Workers
Department for Education and Employment
Sanctuary Buildings
Great Smith Street
London SW1P 3BT
Tel: 0171-925 5000

METRA Services Ltd
PO Box 1540
Homer Road
Solihull
West Midlands B91 3QB
Tel: 0121-704 6699

The Carnegie Third Age Programme
3 Robert Street
London WC2N 6BN
Tel: 0171-976 1785

Employers Forum on Age
Astral House
1268 London Road
London SW16 4ER
Tel: 0181-679 1075

The Third Age Challenge Trust
Anglia House
115 Commercial Road
Swindon SW1 5PL
Tel: 01793 533370

Local Government Management Board
38 Belgrave Square
London SW1X 8NZ
Tel: 0171-235 6081

Further Information

Could you use Additional Copies of this Book?

Croner's Guide to Handling Sensitive Issues in the Workplace is a pocketbook designed for practical use by employers who need to deal sensitively with the difficult issues that can arise in the workplace. If you are a subscriber to *Croner's Reference Book for Employers* then this is one of a series of books which are included in your subscription.

Are there any other managers in your organisation who would benefit from this easy-to-read examination of employment law? If so, why not give them a copy to help them consolidate their knowledge. Additional copies at a special price of £8.00 plus £1.50 p&p per copy, may be ordered by telephoning our Customer Services team on 0181-247 1175/1176, quoting reference QFJK.

Training

Attending a seminar is one of the best ways of keeping up with rapidly changing legislation, trends and new ideas. Croner Training has 10 years' experience of running an extensive range of courses, from three day residential to one day seminars, all led by authoritative and experienced speakers. Courses are regularly offered on the following subjects:

Drafting Contracts of Employment
The Effective Personnel Assistant
Advanced Employment Law
Psychometric Tests: Their Selection and Use
Managing Sickness Absence
Going to Tribunal

Payroll Management
Statutory Sick Pay
Maternity and Equal Opportunities
Employment Law Update
Introduction to Pensions.

For further information on any of these courses please contact Croner Training on 0181-547 3333, quoting reference CXDD.

Croner In-Company Training

Courses offered on:
Employment Law
Management Skills
Health and Safety
Dangerous Substances
Importing/Exporting
VAT and Finance

and many more tailored to your needs, for all levels of staff, anywhere in Europe.

Our package comprises:

- participative, tailored course
- no-obligation preliminary meeting
- full back-up documentation
- experienced and practical trainers
- competitive price, estimated in advance
- backed by the Croner reputation.

For details of value for money, affordable courses for four or more staff, tailored to your needs, please contact Claire Spraggs on 0181-547 3333, quoting reference NZDM.

Croner Information Services

The current range of our information packages includes the following.

NEW Croner's Employee Relations — This package covers all the information you need to know about the existing and coming employee relations policies and laws. The European influence regarding these measures is already being felt. Keep up with individual employee relations developments and have your organisation properly prepared before they happen.

NEW Croner's Recruitment, Selection and Induction — This information service follows the initial stages of the employment cycle, with the emphasis on best practice in these important areas.

Croner's Reference Book For Employers — Known as the "Personnel Manager's Bible", this service covers all the legal obligations you face as an employer, in clear, precise, "jargon free" language.

Croner's Employment Law — An authoritative and comprehensive reference service covering the complex area of employment law, keeping you abreast of all the legislative changes, developments in courts and the European law, affecting the rights of individual employees.

Croner's Flexible Working Practices — A completely new essential reference service for all personnel professionals and general managers responsible for planning and implementing new working methods.

Croner's Discrimination Law — A new loose-leaf reference book to help personnel professionals guide their company through the complex world of discrimination law, including a detailed chapter on the Disability Discrimination Act.

Croner's Training and Development Information Service — A completely new information service which comprises three package components:
- The Directory of Management Training Resources
- The Monthly Briefing

- The Looseleaf Reference Guide, providing practical guidelines to customised training, the various concepts of training, and development strategies for businesses.

Croner's Personnel In Practice — A detailed reference source of tried and tested practical forms and procedures together with the UK's leading employment newsletter.

Croner's Pay And Benefits Sourcebook — Essential reading for anyone involved in designing salary packages and pay policy in a company.

Croner's Personnel Assistant's Handbook — Covering all the main areas of personnel, including interviewing and report-writing skills, employment law contracts, recruitment and selection, health and safety and much more. It is also an essential study guide for the Certificate in Personnel Practice course.

Croner's Team Leader's Briefing — A fortnightly newsletter containing articles and advice on the day-to-day problems and issues which the team leader or supervisor faces.

Croner's Industrial Relations Law — An authoritative guide on all the legal provisions which regulate the relationship between employer and trade union members and trade unions.

Croner's Employment Case Law Index — Structured to keep the busy personnel professional up-to-date and locate relevant facts and summaries of findings for significant cases.

Croner's A–Z Guide for HRM Professionals — Providing information on a wide spectrum of human resource management and organisational issues to enable the identification, planning and implementation of a business-led HR strategy.

Croner's Employment Law for Local Authority Employers — A practical guide for local authority personnel and line managers concentrating on all aspects of employment legislation specifically affecting local government, including special provisions and implications of major policy issues.

Croner's Employment Law Line — A telephone advisory service which is specially designed to provide guidance with your difficult and individual employment-related problems.

For further information, please contact our Customer Services team on 0181-247 1175/1176.

INDEX

F

G

H

J

K

L

M

S